Unforgettable
journeys to take
before you die

Unforgettable
journeys to take
before you die

Steve Watkins and Clare Jones

CONTENTS

Introduction

It is said that even a journey of a thousand miles begins with a single step, but nowadays it seems that many journeys can begin with something as simple as the click of a computer mouse. Blanket media coverage of travel and, perhaps more significantly, the internet have revolutionized our access to information about almost every destination on the planet, no matter how remote. We could be forgiven for thinking we have seen places and know all about them without ever leaving the comfort of our homes.

For some, the option to travel is not there and glimpsing the world through the eyes of others provides the next best thing. The truth, though, is that no matter how much web surfing you do, how many magazines, books or newspapers you read, or how many television travel shows you watch, there is no substitute for actually taking a journey yourself.

Whether you choose to take an icy voyage across the southern seas of Antarctica to bring to life the remarkable story of Ernest Shackleton and the crew of HMS *Endurance*, or perhaps go deep into the Rwandan jungle to track mountain gorillas, the experience of being there will far outstrip any preconceived ideas. No photograph can capture the bracing chill of a katabatic wind as it sweeps down from the heights of a deep-blue glacier, or convey the wonder of sitting beside a female gorilla who is cradling her newborn baby as a human would. As photographers, we can only hope to come close.

Knowing that this book could fall into the category of 'blanket media coverage', we have tried to place it somewhere between that and actually being there. We hope we have provided an enjoyable bridge of inspiration, in images and words, that will encourage you to explore a new place, choose a different type of holiday or finally book that dream trip. As with the other books in the *Unforgettable* series, we have tried, above all, to keep a sense of reality. The journeys we describe are available to anyone, and we took our photographs on the hoof. We simply didn't have time to wait for days or weeks in the same spot for just the right light, much as we may have wanted to.

Researching, organizing and travelling for this book has been both challenging and immensely rewarding. If the experiences of the people we've met along the way are anything to go by, many readers will have already made one or several of the journeys described here – some lucky ones may have done most of them, and more besides. And everyone will have their own personal favourite journey that didn't make it into these pages. Our fellow travellers certainly did, and the sometimes heated discussions we enjoyed with them showed us that the spirit of adventure, and the inherent human desire to journey and explore, are well and truly alive.

It seems, too, that there is an ever-growing collective consciousness of just how fragile and already scarred the Earth is, and how it is our pressing responsibility to ensure that its wild and beautiful places and creatures are protected. We cannot justify tourism if that tourism is itself one of the factors that is endangering the very sights we wish to see. If we want to travel in ever-greater numbers, we have to accept increasingly managed and controlled interactions with our destinations. Thankfully, the organizations that govern tourist activities understand this and are working hard to strike the right balance between conservation and delivering an unforgettable experience. It can be achieved, but it helps if we, as travellers, take our share of the responsibility and go with a flexible mindset and a light tread. It is easy to understand the disappointment if that elusive lion or polar bear just isn't synchronizing with your often costly itinerary. However, demanding guaranteed encounters and experiences puts increasing pressure on tour operators to compromise their environmental and conservation standards – the start of an inevitable downward spiral. Our actions count and have a substantial impact; there is no better time than this to realize that it is the journey itself, both physical and mental, with its inherent uncertainty, that is the destination.

For this book we wanted to include not just classic journeys, such as Route 66 or the Camino de Santiago, but also lesser-known ones, such as following the reindeer migration with the Sámi people of northern Sweden and a horse-riding safari in Botswana. The list is in no way definitive, and neither is it ordered in any sort of ranking priority. The map on pages 252–3 shows the locations of all the journeys featured.

Among our many memories, the ones that stand out most are perhaps the less obvious ones. Waking up on the Patagonian ice cap in a small tent that was being battered by ferocious winds (an alarm call that deserves to be ignored) and, on finding the courage to leave our warm sleeping bags, poking our heads out to be greeted by the most glorious orange, red and blue light show dancing across the granite spires of the Fitz Roy Massif – a fleeting moment that would have been so easy to miss. Talking to a fellow passenger in Antarctica who, eight years earlier, had been given three months to live by doctors, yet refused to accept the inevitable and found ways to overcome his illness, deciding there and then to grasp every opportunity to do what he had always wanted to do in life. The woman in Canada who, instead of flying, took the arduous, two-day train journey back from Churchill to Winnipeg to retrace the route her mother had taken decades earlier. Travelling has never been so accessible; but the journeys we undertake are still as personal, challenging and fulfilling as they were on the day Shackleton set sail on *Endurance*.

Steve Watkins and Clare Jones, 2006

Riding the Okavango Delta

Botswana

Evening ride on the flood plain

Riding a horse through the flood waters of Botswana's immense Okavango Delta, close to elephants, giraffes and the odd lion or two, must rank as one of the world's most exhilarating wildlife journeys.

The difference between being on horseback and in a safari vehicle may seem minor compared to the awe that seeing animals in their natural habitat inspires, but in the saddle you are most certainly part of the scene and not just a spectator. This extra edge of excitement may well re-awaken in you something of our primal past, taking you back for an instant to the time of our hunter-gatherer ancestors.

An exhilarating canter through the delta's shallow water

There are many places to go on safari in Africa, but the Okavango Delta in Botswana is held in particularly high regard because it is relatively untouched by humans and is, as a result, teeming with big game. Hundreds of elephants are thought to roam the area, as well as lions, cheetahs, panthers, wild dogs, giraffes, hippos and a raft of other supporting wildlife stars.

The delta, to the west of Maun in the north of landlocked Botswana, is formed by the Cubango and Cuito rivers, which flow out of the Angolan highlands before merging to create the Okavango river. When it reaches flat land it slows to a creep and fans out into myriad shallow channels, bringing an explosion of green life to the

semi-desert. Thousands of low-lying islands are created, providing dry ground for wildlife and a pitching spot for several luxury safari camps, including Macatoo, the base for this adventure into the delta.

A 30-minute flight from Maun airport in a small Cessna, Macatoo Camp is perched on the edge of one of the main channels, and offers spectacular sunset-watching from its sun deck – plus, if you are lucky, some very up-close-and-personal visits from big game. With a large stable of excellent horses, professional guides to lead the rides

Giraffes can be surprisingly well camouflaged

Flocks of cranes arrive with the flood water

Nervous impala

Riding allows very close wildlife encounters

and a host of support workers, the camp rightly has an enviable reputation for providing a great riding experience. It's not all about the horses either – good food, served in the open air, and large luxury tents that could easily be considered suites, also help to make this a truly memorable three- or four-day safari.

Rides twice a day mean it is easy to explore deep into the delta. The morning one, when the guides take you to beautiful, shallow lakes full of water lilies where you can canter your horse, tends to be

Long grasses cover the delta

the more active of the two. It is unlike any other riding experience. With rainbows forming in the splashing water around you and the thud of huge drops of water bouncing off your body and face, it is truly exhilarating. The horses love it, too, and have to be held back a little to stop them galloping off to the horizon. You will get wet – very wet – but the warm Botswana sun will quickly have you dry again.

In between canters you are very likely to encounter big game. On horseback it is possible to get quite close to elephants, giraffes and many other animals, as they do not perceive the horses as a threat. The sense of drama, and tension levels, rise immeasurably though, as does your heart rate, as you edge closer to them, your guide ever aware of the need to maintain a respectful distance. It is as different to being in a safari vehicle as riding a motorbike is to being in a car.

Expect to get wet during the rides

The evening rides are even more spectacular than the morning ones, though usually more sedate, with golden light streaming across the grassy delta and the animals coming out to eat and drink. It is a magical time, and as the sun's rays filter through the dust kicked up by the horses the romance of Africa comes to life. Back at the camp you can kick off your boots, sip a gin and tonic on the sun deck and watch the occasional giraffe or elephant wander by. The more active might like to take a boat trip down the channel – a refreshing way to see the sun go down.

Flood waters creep across the delta

As you sit round the lamp-lit dinner table, feasting on excellent food and wine, listening for any tell-tale sounds of animals roaming

RIDING THE OKAVANGO DELTA

Tranquil waters at Macatoo Camp

Fine outdoor dining at Macatoo

Riding the delta at end of day

into the camp and looking back on your day, you will find it hard to deny that a horseback safari is as close as you will ever come to answering the call of the wild.

ⓘ ....

Several operators, including African Horseback Safaris, owners of Macatoo Camp, run horse-riding safaris in the Okavango Delta. You need to be a fairly experienced rider, primarily because the horses may bolt when surprised by animals in the bush. You can stay at the camp for three or four nights, or longer. Several agents, including Tim Best Travel, will arrange flights to Botswana with British Airways or other airlines, and help to organize domestic transfers to Maun. Flights to Macatoo Camp from Maun will be arranged by African Horseback Safaris.

Sunset over the delta from Macatoo Camp

If you crave the vast, snow-filled landscape of the North or South Pole but would prefer not to come face-to-face with pack ice, or even a polar bear, Argentina's *campo de hielo sur* (southern ice cap), also affectionately called the 'third pole', offers an alternative 'polar' extreme – and a step back in time. Here, what lies underfoot is age-old ice, 1000 metres thick. Trekking on it provides a view of the world as it was 10,000 years ago at the end of the last ice age.

Climbing the Marconi Glacier towards Marconi Pass

Over 350 km long, the southern ice cap is the largest body of non-polar ice on earth, the third biggest glacier mass after Antarctica and Greenland. And getting on to it is a journey in itself that takes you into Patagonia's Los Glaciares national park. Hiking through tranquil, unspoilt beech forests and past tumbling waterfalls and glacier-fed streams, you eventually reach what appears to be a never-ending sea of ice.

Patagonia spans two countries, Argentina and Chile, and covers almost 800,000 sq. km. Its landscape is dominated by mountains, glaciers, dramatically hewn valleys and wide sprawling plains. On the

Ice cap trek
Patagonia, Argentina

Deep crevasses fracture the Marconi Glacier

Scree litters the lower glacier

Chilean side it begins south of the city of Puerto Montt and in Argentina south of the Colorado River. Separating the two countries, and rising steeply above the steppe lands, are the majestic, snow-capped Andes mountains. From these come tumbling the many huge glaciers that feed the region's distinctive green-blue lakes. Patagonia ends at Tierra del Fuego, literally the 'end of the world' and the southernmost extreme of the Americas.

The bustling town of El Calafate is a gateway to many of the popular adventure activities in southern Patagonia, and a starting point for a trek to the ice cap. From here a five-hour journey on a mainly rough road leads eventually to the burgeoning town of El Chaltén, on the edge of the Los Glaciares national park. En route, across the sprawling open plains, roaming llama-like guanacos, remote *estancias* or farms, and the odd gaucho on horseback may be the only signs of life.

Once simply a remote border outpost with nothing more than a scattering of buildings, El Chaltén has become a base camp for expeditions into the surrounding peaks of the Fitz Roy Massif, where towering granite monoliths stand more than 1500 metres high. While its main street is still a dirt track where horses and hikers roam equally freely and the distinctive Patagonian wind can whip the dust into spiralling clouds like something out of a spaghetti western, modern facilities, including small hostels, restaurants and a couple of basic shops, make it a comfortable resting place before you head for the ice.

The trail head is about a 20-minute drive out of town. Here a small wooden sign points along a tumbling river towards windswept beech forests and the campsite of Piedra del Fraile (the Monk's Stone). At this starting point you can look straight down the valley to the snow-capped peaks in the distance and the route that leads upwards to the ice. A gentle two-hour hike brings you to the campsite, an easy goal for a lunch stop on day one.

From here you head into more open scenery, along the river fed by Lago Eléctrica, and the terrain becomes a bit more testing as the trail

Rest break on Marconi Glacier

Guides are essential on the glacier

Ropes provide protection from crevasse falls

Mount Fitz Roy at sunset

Fitz Roy Massif at sunset

Camp over the Marconi Glacier

Fiery sunrise

begins to weave through a canyonland of glaciated bedrock. Look out for Andean condors riding the warm thermals above – their arcing flight will be a restful distraction.

Surrounded as you are by towering mountains, finding out that you are heading for the beach (La Playita) may seem slightly out of context. But the first night's camp is so named for its sandy position on the edge of a river plain. A soft spot for some well-earned sleep.

The onward journey to the ice cap starts in earnest the following day when you strap on crampons for the first time and step on to the lower reaches of the Marconi Glacier. From a distance it looks like wind-blown ice cream, but once you have trekked up from the previous night's camp this apparent softness disappears. You find yourself in a refrigerated maze where you have to pick a route through obstacles that include ice-carved bridges, and cavernous holes so deep that just one carelessly chosen footing means you would be swallowed up.

Like an icy mane of hair, the glacier cascades downwards. As you begin to weave through its swathe of frozen locks, it gradually swings to the right revealing a view that has remained out of sight for almost two days. The ice rears steeply into what looks like a sheer wall guarded on either side by steeper, impassable ice cliffs, where overhanging snow collects in huge bundles, like oversized marshmallows waiting to fall and bounce their way down the glacier. Above sits the Paso Marconi (Marconi Pass), the gateway to the ice cap.

A way up and over this wall-like feature has to be chosen carefully, but quickly. The skills of your guide will be invaluable in assessing the safety of the route and the danger of an avalanche from the precipitously perched snow above. Up close, though, the terrain is far easier and less demanding than it looks from a distance and while you have to be roped to your guide no technical climbing is required. However, carrying an ice axe is essential to stop you in the event of a fall. A short but concentrated effort will see you through this area, the most challenging section of the route.

Sweeping view over the Southern Patagonia Ice Field

Once you have reached the pass a short trek takes you to where the glacier opens wide into a vast ice blanket, its surface hewn by crevasses. Even though the views so far have been spectacular, this sublime white wilderness has a jaw-dropping quality that will surpass your expectations. After only two days of trekking, you are looking out on a seemingly endless sea of ice, as wild as it is wide.

ⓘ ....

Buenos Aires-based Oyikil Viajes can organize short treks to the ice cap and also offer a nine-day tour that allows you to traverse the ice cap in a circular route from El Chaltén via the Marconi Glacier to the Viedma Glacier. The season runs from October through to April. Previous experience with crampons, snowshoes and mountaineering skis is not required as guidance is provided. The company does request camping and trekking experience, and participants must be prepared to be self-sufficient in setting up camps and preparing meals. The terrain is demanding, and adequate training and preparation are required, along with a high level of fitness. Journey Latin America is one of several companies that can arrange flights to Argentina.

Each step needs care around crevasse fields

Along the Gibb River Road
Kimberley, Australia

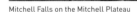

Mitchell Falls on the Mitchell Plateau

No visit down under is complete without venturing into the outback, the vast inhospitable central area that pushes almost all Australians to live on the continent's coastal fringes. For many travellers the outback is Australia, and one of the region's most exciting drives is along the remote Gibb River Road in the Kimberley region of Western Australia.

Stretching for 647 km from Derby, just north of Broome on the west coast, to Kununurra on the state border with the Northern Territory, the Gibb River Road takes about a week to traverse by car, allowing you time to stop and savour the wild and enchanting space that is the outback. En route, you can stay at traditional cattle stations, now

Four-wheel-drive vehicles are essential

offering comfortable homestay accommodation, spend a night or two in an authentic canvas swag bed under the stars, and see great waterfalls and rarely visited Aboriginal rock-art sites.

On leaving Derby the first place worth exploring is Windjana Gorge, across the Napier Downs, where the asphalted section of the road ends. This is the land of the cattle drovers, and the gorge was once the site of a stock camp to which up to 500 head of cattle at a time were driven. Sliced from the rock by the Lennard River, its 90-metre-high walls are part of what was once the prehistoric Devonian reef system, and archaeologists have discovered fossils of long-extinct creatures high up in the red cliff faces.

Lennard River

Windjana Gorge

Further east, through the King Leopold Range National Park, is the first of the homestays: Mount Hart. With a 50-km 'driveway' from the main track, just getting to its front door gives an insight into how vast the outback is. When the folk there talk of their neighbours it is likely they are describing people several hours away by car, yet the bond between them seems as strong as if they all lived on a housing estate. Everyone in this wilderness is a big character, and Mount Hart owner Taffy Abbots is one of the biggest. 'The shops are only 250 kilometres away if you have forgotten something,' he quipped on our arrival.

One of Taffy's closest neighbours – almost 200 km away – is Michael Kerr at the next homestay along the track: Old Mornington Station. Situated south of the main Gibb River Road, this is a 1-million-acre property, which is still working cattle. The main attraction, though, is Dimond Gorge, where you can paddle the tranquil waters in an open canoe. With its red rock walls rising around you, it is, for a moment at least, easy to imagine you are one of the hardy pioneers who opened up this remote part of Australia.

A relatively recent discovery in a far-flung corner of Old Mornington is an ancient Aboriginal rock-art site, where comets streak across the walls and traditional ancestor Wandjina figures, with their spiky hair, stare down from the roof of the cave. It is a moving reminder that European pioneers were merely following in the footsteps of the Aboriginal people who have lived here for around 40,000 years.

Back on the main track, the driving is exhilarating as you rattle over the bumps with not a care in the world, save for avoiding the odd dingo crossing the road or the occasional road train thundering past. Road trains are the three-trailer monsters of the outback, and they are both awesome and terrifying as they billow dust on their

Driving across Napier Downs

On the track to Dimond Gorge

unstoppable mission to deliver goods to remote communities. Pulling aside and watching is always the best way to deal with them.

After an overnight stop at Drysdale River Station, on a branch track off the main road, it is worth spending a day or two continuing north up the track towards Kalumburu and the incredible Mitchell Plateau. The Gibb River Road may be isolated, but the narrower and rougher Kalumburu Road, and then the Port Warrender Road, take you further still, so put on your explorer's cap and go prepared to camp. Your reward will be a view of one of Australia's most

Remote bush telephone box, Windjana Gorge

Previous pages: Ord River near Kununurra

Canoeing in Dimond Gorge

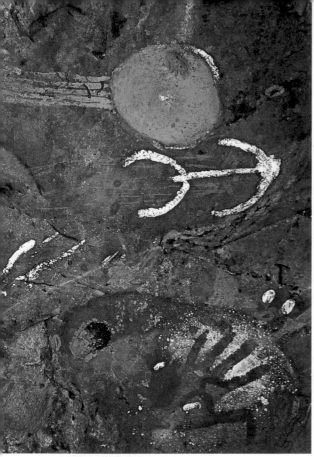

Aboriginal cave paintings at Old Mornington

Trekking in the gorges below Mitchell Falls

breathtakingly picturesque waterfalls: the three-tiered Mitchell Falls. In season, taking a helicopter flight from the campsite is easily the best way to see them.

Back on the Gibb River Road, it is a real last-night treat to stop short of Kununurra at El Questro Wilderness Park, an ecotourism station and brainchild of an English millionaire. It may seem truly wild to anyone who has simply come from Kununurra, but after your journey along the magical Gibb River Road it will be the height of luxury.

Monitor lizard at Mitchell Falls

ⓘ ....

Many airlines, including Qantas, fly to Australia's main gateway cities. Qantas also offer domestic flights to Broome. It is essential to hire a four-wheel-drive vehicle to travel the Gibb River Road. Several rental companies, including Hertz, have offices at Broome airport. Carry sufficient supplies of water, food and spare fuel in case of emergency – you may have to wait several days for another vehicle to pass by if yours breaks down. And ask the rental company to supply two spare tyres with your vehicle.

Canal du Midi
France

Trees enclose many parts of the canal, such as at Trebes

Poppies line the canal

Flying the tricolore at Le Somail

Stretching halfway across southern France from Toulouse to Agde, and part of the link between the Atlantic Ocean and the Mediterranean Sea, the Canal du Midi is one of Europe's greatest engineering feats. Navigating its tree-lined, gentle waters takes you through landscapes, villages and towns that are quintessentially French.

Masterminded by Pierre Paul-Riquet, more than twelve thousand men were employed in its construction, which began in 1666. It was inaugurated in 1681. So impressive was the achievement, and so important is the canal to the heartbeat of the region, that it has recently been given UNESCO World Heritage status. Starting from Toulouse, where it joins the Canal Latéral à la Garonne, which comes from the Atlantic Ocean, it twists and turns for 240 km through the beautiful rolling countryside of Languedoc-Rousillon to Bassin de

Thau, near Agde, on the Mediterranean coast. Once an important trading route, which replaced a 3000-km voyage around the south of Spain, the canal is now the preserve of travellers aboard barges and pleasure cruisers. Some people have made it their home, but most come on holiday to spend a week or so plying its waters.

Winding through the country near Capestang

From Toulouse, it passes through the delightful town of Castelnaudary, where houses roofed with terracotta tiles rise majestically out of the water to the crowning glory of the cathedral with its tall spire. This is the heart of Cathar country, where the heretical sect spread its religion in opposition to the Church of Rome at the end of the 11th century. It was crushed in a series of brutal massacres during the 20-year Albigensian Crusade led by Simon de Montfort, and later persecuted by the Inquisition. Cathar castles dot the ridges and hilltops in several towns of the region and are well worth visiting.

Heading further east, the canal gently winds its way through open country and a series of locks, including a picturesque, tree-lined one at Bram. Most of them offer a chance to take a coffee break and the

Café at Le Somail

larger ones are good overnight mooring spots. After Bram, in the broad reaches of the Aude valley, lies one of the gems of the entire journey: the spectacular medieval walled city of Carcassonne with its fairy-tale ramparts. The canal runs into its adjacent modern area – an ideal place to stop for a couple of days at least. La Cité, the old part of the city, is protected by an imposing double ring of walls that features 52 towers and is deservedly on UNESCO's World Heritage list.

From Carcassonne, the canal follows the path of the Aude River, taking you through quintessential French terrain where vineyards stretch to the horizon and long, regimented stretches of plane, poplar and cypress trees line its banks. Apart from looking pretty, the trees provide shade, which in turn significantly reduces evaporation, and

Classic French country house at La Croisade

A houseboat at Villeneuve-lès-Béziers

PORT DU SOMAIL
À 12096 MÈT.   À 13343 MÈT.
DU PONT   DE L'ÉCLUSE
DE PIGASSE.   D'ARGENS.

BRAM.
CONTRÔLE INTERMÉDIAIRE
DES DROITS DE NAVIGATION.
DISTANCES:
DE L'ÉCLUSE   DE L'ÉCLUSE
DE BETEILLE.   DE BRAM.
4962 MÈTRES.   630 MÈTRES.

AUX MILLE PAINS

ÉCLUSE DE FONFILE
DISTANCES:
DE L'ÉCLUSE   DE L'ÉCLUSE
DE MARSEILLETTE DE St MARTIN
3308 MÈTRES.   1242 MÈTRES

Canal west of Capestang

Radiating fields at Etang de Montady

also strengthen the banks. After negotiating the locks at Trebes, around 8 km out of Carcassonne, the canal returns to open country and you may make it to the village of Puicheric by the end of day.

You will probably enjoy the most memorable moments of your journey in one of the many tiny villages you pass through. Once the canal has left the Aude River and ventured further north, the village of Le Somail awaits with its enchanting ivy-covered lock-keeper's cottage, old medieval church and a couple of excellent waterside restaurants. A glass of fine Languedoc red wine is a perfect dinner companion as you enjoy the tranquillity and watch ducks waddling on the cobbled towpath.

From Le Somail, the canal snakes effortlessly towards La Croisade then on to Capestang – prosperous during the Middle Ages, the town still retains a vestige of its former glory in the commanding collegiate church that dominates the landscape for miles around. Soon after passing Poilhes, you will skirt the southern edges of the Etang de Montady, a plain famed for its radiating fields. From the sleepy village of Montady, high on a nearby hill, they look like slices of

La Cité at Carcassonne

a large pie. The last big population centre on the canal is the lively city of Béziers, about 5 km further east, where the cathedral of Saint-Nazaire is the highlight.

The Mediterranean Sea beckons, and for the last day or so the canal takes you across a flat coastal plain – at times running arrow-straight to the horizon – to the old port of Agde. With its fleet of colourful fishing boats, it is known as the 'black pearl of the Mediterranean' and is a fitting end to a voyage along the Canal du Midi.

Old men chatting at Castelnaudary

ⓘ ··

Several international airlines fly directly to Toulouse. Numerous companies, based in Toulouse and other villages and towns along the canal, hire out boats ranging from modern motor cruisers to traditional old barges, for periods that can last from as little as one day to several weeks. Traffic levels on the canal can be a little intimidating for novice boat-handlers during the peak summer months of July and August, so try to travel at some other time if possible – the canal is open year round. You don't need a licence to hire a boat, and the hire company will give you lessons in vessel control. If you prefer to leave the stress of driving to someone else, larger barges with professional pilots are available. Most boats are hired out on a self-catering basis.

Driving along Route 66
Arizona, USA

Rolling hills near Seligman

Hackberry gas station

Dubbed 'America's Main Street', Route 66 crosses the country from Chicago to Los Angeles and is probably the world's most famous road. Interstate highways have replaced many parts of the old route but the spirit of 66 is still alive and kicking, and one of the best ways to get a true taste of it is to drive the original section between Williams and Topock across the wild expanses of Arizona.

The story of Route 66, all 3600 km or so of it across eight states, is infused with the characters, landscapes, lifestyles and even songs that epitomized the Great American Dream of the 1940s through to the 1960s. Given its official name in 1926, the road soon after gave

Twisters Soda Fountain

Road sign in Williams

passage to the large-scale migration of Midwestern farmers and their families fleeing drought for the lure of California – immortalized in John Steinbeck's Pulitzer-Prize-winning book *The Grapes of Wrath*.

It took until 1937 for the entire route to be paved – the first cross-country highway to be completed – and it was only after the end of the Second World War that the road really caught the imagination of the American public. With car ownership soaring, Route 66 became a favourite holiday drive; and California continued to be a magnet for people who were looking to change their lives after returning from the war. Songwriter Bobby Troup was doing just that, heading for the bright lights of Los Angeles, when in 1946 he wrote the now legendary 'Get Your Kicks on Route 66' – just try not singing it as you're driving along the road.

On the verge of being buried under the new network of interstate highways in the 1980s, the old road has recently experienced a strong

Corvette at Hackberry gas station

revival. There are original sections in most of the states, but Arizona is home to the longest continuous section. Some 40 km west of Flagstaff is the small town of Williams. Gateway to the not-to-be-missed Grand Canyon just over an hour's drive or train ride north, its streets are lined with classic 1950s diners, gas stations and soda shops. Walking into Twisters Soda Fountain, with its pink Cadillac parked outside and interior filled with chrome fixtures, is like stepping back to a time when nobody hurried, everybody chatted and the days slipped by as easily as the ice-cream sodas and fresh coffee slipped down.

With your car windows wound down and some good old, steering-wheel-thumping rock and roll music on the radio, set off west to the nearby village of Ash Fork, where Route 66 says goodbye to Interstate 40 for almost 260 km. Immediately, the stresses of driving begin to ease as the relatively traffic-free old highway begins to stretch its way

Old gas bowser, Seligman

across the open plains and low-lying hills towards Seligman. Every now and again a Harley-Davidson, with its deep, window-rattling roar, will pass you, the wind flowing through the hair of its almost invariably heavily suntanned rider. It is an *Easy Rider* image of freedom, adventure and the seemingly eternal American Dream that somewhere along the road there is a better life.

Seligman is an iconic Route 66 town, rising out of the plain and consisting of one overly wide main street and a host of classic diners, motels and general stores. Old Chevrolets, Cadillacs and Ford Dodge trucks line the way or can be seen, rusty, parked in backyards. Seligman is also home to Angel Delgadillo, the town's now-retired barber and one of the most fervent campaigners to revive the mother road – he founded the association to preserve it as Historic Route 66. His barbershop, with its walls decked out with the business cards of clients, is an attraction for all who pass by. If you stop overnight at the Historic Route 66 Motel somebody famous, whether a Motown

Angel Delgadillo's barber chair

The renowned barbershop in Seligman

artist or a Hollywood actor, is almost certain to have stayed in your room before you.

Further west, the old highway passes through magnificent undulating country where sweeping views open up at every crest on this roller-coaster drive. At the characterful Hackberry gas station, every surface is decorated with Route 66 memorabilia. The rusty wreck of a very old Ford leads on to the seductive lines of the owner's red-and-white Corvette up front. Neon signs light up the forecourt while behind the station a fascinating collection of old pick-ups and other dilapidated cars reflects the glory of Route 66's heyday.

As beguiling as the open road is, perhaps the most classic section of Route 66 lies ahead to the south-west of Kingman. Soon after leaving the town, easily the biggest on this continuous stretch, the old highway begins to climb into the Black Mountains towards Oatman, a quirky Wild West gold-mining village straight out of a B-movie western. The narrow and precipitous road twists, curves and

snakes its way upwards and demands the utmost concentration. In the early days of Route 66, when brakes overheated and power steering wasn't even a pipe dream, there were drivers who found this section so frightening that they hired locals to drive it for them. It is exhilarating. En route several parking spots allow you to stop and admire the stunning views.

Oatman itself, with its creaky wooden walkways and restaurants, gift shops and lopsided saloons, was one of the first Route 66 villages to be bypassed by a new interstate highway. These days its most famous inhabitants are the wild donkeys that wander the street looking cute in an attempt to solicit food from travellers, although feeding them is prohibited. As the road begins its long descent out of the mountains towards Topock on the California border, the

Twisting route through the Black Mountains to Oatman

Heading to the Black Mountains from Kingman

landscape becomes dry and is dotted with cacti. The other traffic is even less frequent and you can slide your elbow out of the window, crank up the volume on your stereo and sing along to 'Get Your Kicks on Route 66' all the way to the sunshine coast.

ⓘ ···

Driving the entire length of Route 66 would take at least three weeks and allow only minimal time to see places en route. The Arizona section from Williams to Topock could be done in a couple of days, but it is worth spending four days or so savouring places along the road and heading up to the Grand Canyon. Although there are gas stations, make sure you plan your fuel stops to avoid running dry, especially on the section from Kingman to Topock. There are plenty of motels along the way for accommodation. If you have a motorbike licence, several companies in the region rent out Harley-Davidsons.

Following the reindeer migration
Lapland, Sweden

Lap dogs are small but effective reindeer herders

Riding pillion on a skidoo while trying to herd some two hundred reindeer during their spring migration has got to be one of the more exhilarating ways to travel through the vast Arctic tundra. It also allows you to get close to a very special and ancient way of life as you join the indigenous Sámi people on a 200-km journey across Sweden's Lapland. Just like their ancestors before them, they take their animals from the lowland winter feeding grounds through an extraordinary landscape, where frozen lakes, fir trees still laden with winter snow and wide open lowland valleys lead ultimately to mountains and summer pastures.

Neck tags enable wandering females to be monitored

Skidoos are a fun way to travel

The traditional home of the Sámi people, Lapland includes the northernmost parts of Norway, Sweden and Finland, and also the Kola peninsula in Russia. For would-be herders, the migration most typically begins in the small northern town of Gällivare in Sweden, about a three-hour drive south-east of the airport at Kiruna. Here you climb aboard a skidoo then slowly weave your way towards higher ground, fertile grazing and the 1810-metre Kallaktjåkkå mountain, where the first calves are born at the beginning of May. This is part of Stora Sjöfallets (Great Lake Falls) national park, a World Heritage Site.

Keeping away the chills at overnight camp

This journey is an intrinsic part of life for both herders and reindeer, bonding them in a special relationship. Come spring, the animals would naturally begin to head west, instinctively picking a route through snow-filled valleys and upwards to the mountains. However, alone they would be vulnerable to bad weather, lack of food and even attack by predators. For the Sámi, a safe migration is essential as the reindeer are central to their lives, providing them with food and income through the sale of meat and fur – so they head into the tundra to herd the animals on this crucial journey. It is something the Sámi have undertaken for thousands of years and remains a carefully preserved tradition, handed down from generation to generation.

One dominant reindeer always leads the herd

Sámi herders now use skidoos rather than skis

The migration was once an even tougher job than it is today. Before the use of modern skidoos, the herders set out on cross-country skis. Now the distance can be covered much more quickly, but some of the age-old traditions haven't been forgotten – not least where you rest your head in the evening.

You will find yourself bedding down for the night in a *lavu*, the traditional herder's tent, made now of tough canvas rather than reindeer skins and erected on the snow. While this may sound chilly don't be put off – skins cover the floor and are used on top of sleeping bags for extra warmth. It may just begin to get too comfortable, especially when it comes to getting up to help with the early morning job of rounding up the reindeer and collecting food for them. But you can take on as much or as little of the work as you want. The 'real'

Sunset over a *lavu* tent

herders are there, rising early and jumping on to their skidoos to race off and find the reindeer – which don't stay still for long. Following their natural instinct to head west to the mountains, these gentle animals just keep moving.

Even in spring the roots, lichens and moss that they like to feed on remain hidden under snow, so the Sámi collect and lay out food for them, including their favourite *sláhppu*, a wiry moss that grows in tree branches. Before you know it you will probably find yourself wanting to be out there with the herders, doing the work rather than watching from a distance.

Participating fully means bashing branches to get at the moss and frantically flailing and waving your arms as you join in the daily round-up. This is one of the slightly more chaotic parts of the day, when break-away reindeer have to be coerced back into the herd – and the sight of a herder lying flat on his face in the snow after an unsuccessful chase is not unusual. There are people, arms and animals almost everywhere. Then, almost magically, the wonderful, blissful peace is skilfully and sublimely restored and the journey can begin again, across yet more untracked snow.

It's hard not to get drawn into the life of the herd and this migration. Every reindeer has its own unique character, from the toss of a head to the shake of a tail, and the animals become absorbing to watch and get to know. A white reindeer – a particularly rare colouration – is considered spiritually special by the Sámi, and if a family has one it is highly valued.

Each day for a week, as you follow the animals, direct them, regroup them and even guard against the possibility of a wolverine or lynx attack, you become closer to them. And covering ground means getting them to new pastures where they will grow and prosper. The moment when you look out on the herd grazing contentedly on high ground is one you will savour; and the one when you know you have become an honorary reindeer herder.

ⓘ ....

A couple of airlines, including SAS Airlines, fly into Kiruna in Swedish Lapland. The reindeer-migration experience can be organized by Vägvisaren – Pathfinder Lapland, a Sámi family-run ecotourism company set up to provide sustainable tourism in Lapland. Their trips are certified as 'Nature's Best' by the Swedish Eco-tourism Society, whose ecotourism certification system is one of the first in the world. You will need warm clothing for the journey, but outer snow suits and shoes are provided. Traditional Sámi herders will guide and drive you. There may be an opportunity to drive your own skidoo, and full training in driving and herding is given.

Sunset over the western hills

Mysterious, colourful and alluring to early civilizations, the ancient Silk Route that crossed central Asia and the Taklimakan Desert from China to the eastern Mediterranean still provides a sense of real adventure for modern-day travellers. One of the most popular sections takes you from Beijing to Samarkand in Uzbekistan, via Kashgar and Tashkent.

Depending on the number of places you want to stop at en route, the journey can take anything from two weeks to a month or more. Various itineraries are available from tour operators – including ones that allow you to fly and avoid long drives between destinations.

Your first major stop after leaving Beijing is the Great Wall of China. The parts that are easily visited in a day trip from the city are fascinating in themselves, but the ones near Jiayuguan, at the wall's western end and reached a couple of days later by train, are more visually stunning, with pagoda towers spiking a skyline view of snow-capped mountains.

From the Great Wall, a lengthy drive takes you to Gansu Province and Dunhuang, an oasis irrigated by the Tang River and surrounded

The Silk Route
Beijing to Samarkand

Donkey cart in the Flaming Hills, Turpan, China

Camel caravan in the Taklimakan Desert

Women in Kashgar

by the Qilian mountains. Nearby is a labyrinth of outstanding grottoes with Buddhist shrines and scriptures, and superb wall paintings, primarily of battle scenes. Also close by are the Singing Sands – so called because sliding down the dunes creates an eerie whistling sound – where the oasis meets the desert and camel caravans still ply their trade. Dunhuang was the meeting point for two branches of the Silk Route that skirted the north and south edges of the daunting Taklimakan Desert, which stretches to the west.

The Taklimakan (rough translation: Place of No Return) in China's Xinjiang region is as forbidding as it was when the routes were first used. Hemmed in on its northern flank by the mighty Tian Shan mountains and in the south by the Kunlun range, this vast desert covers 270,000 sq. km and is second only to the Sahara in size. Save for the oasis towns around its edges, it is uninhabited and virtually uninhabitable – although recent discoveries of oil may change that.

The northern and southern routes converge again at the oasis of Kashgar. Situated about 200 km from China's border with Kyrgyzstan, the city is home to a large population of Uighur people, whose empire once stretched from Manchuria to the waters of the Caspian Sea. If you arrive there on a Sunday, don't miss the large and colourful market – farmers from miles around come to it to sell their fruit and vegetables.

From Kashgar, it is a long drive up into the Tian Shan mountains over the Torugart Pass, at 3752 metres, and on to the city of Naryn in Kyrgyzstan. Formerly part of the Soviet Union, the region boasts truly spectacular landscapes. Snow-topped mountains stand guard over sweeping grassy plains dotted with magnificent lakes like the vast Issyk-Kul. Life here has changed little over the centuries and horse-drawn carts are still the most popular form of transport outside the

The modern, paved Silk Route

The Silk Route passes through stunning country in Kyrgyzstan

The dunes at Bulun-Kul, Xinjiang, China

more modern capital, Bishkek. Once a caravan stop on the Silk Route, this is now a classic Soviet-style city, and is notable for its wide public spaces and boulevards. Numerous reminders of its recent history include statues of Lenin; Kyrgyzstan became independent in 1991.

Another long drive takes you from Bishkek to Osh on the border of Uzbekistan, and on to Tashkent, the Uzbek capital. An enthralling city and one of the oldest in central Asia, it was a major crossroads where different branches of the Silk Route met. Many of its ancient buildings were destroyed during the Russian Revolution of 1917, but the imposing Soviet buildings that replaced them are still of interest. Beyond the Soviet architecture there are ornate mosques, including the Khast Imam Mosque, which houses the world's oldest Koran.

Further west, Bukhara is one of the region's most visited attractions. Its Kalyan minaret was built in about 1127 and withstood years of conflict, including the Mongol invasion in the 13th century. It's worth climbing its 105 steps for the panoramic views of the city. The emir's palace, the Ark, is also of interest, partly because of its gory history of torture and executions.

Stone farmhouse in the Karakoram Mountains

Stormy sky in the Karakoram Mountains

The gem of the Silk Route is Samarkand, an ideal place to end your journey. Its skyline is strewn with domes and minarets and it would be possible to spend a week just wandering its streets. The highlight of the city is undoubtedly the Registan, a square surrounded by three massive and dazzling madrasas: Tilla-Kari, Shir Dor and Ulug Beg. Another don't-miss sight is the Shah-I-Zinda (Tomb of the Living King).

Even Alexander the Great was overwhelmed by Samarkand's beauty, and it has inspired poets throughout the centuries. When you arrive here after your journey from Beijing you will find it easy, even today, to sense the relief and excitement the traders who travelled the Silk Route would have felt when they reached this magical city.

ⓘ ....

If your time is limited, it is possible to find tours that cover only parts of the route, especially ones that focus solely on the sites in Uzbekistan. There are scheduled flights to Beijing and to Tashkent, but other cities on the Silk Route may be less well served. Be sure to check the visa situation if you are travelling between several countries in central Asia and China, as you may need to apply for one before travelling. Accommodation options vary along the route, but all the major stop-off cities have a reasonable range.

Tracking mountain gorillas
Parc National des Volcans, Rwanda

View from Virunga Lodge

Trekking high up on volcanic slopes in the dense bamboo forests of the Parc National des Volcans (Volcanoes National Park) in Rwanda's Virunga massif, you may have the privilege of meeting one of our closest living relatives: the mountain gorillas. Catapulted into the limelight by the work of Dian Fossey, these animals are highly endangered and coming face to face with them is among the most highly prized and moving wildlife encounters on the planet.

Sign at the park's head office

Trekking towards Sabinyo volcano

Getting to see the gorillas' kingdom is an adventure in itself, as you travel deep into Central Africa from Rwanda's capital, Kigali, to the region where the country's northern border connects with Uganda and the Democratic Republic of Congo (DRC). Thankfully, Rwanda is now well on the road to recovering from the terrible genocide that scarred it so deeply in the mid-1990s. The renewed peace and stability allow you to see the real nature of its people, who invariably greet visitors with big smiles, excited waves and the endearing cry 'Misungu!'

Once you arrive in Kigali it is a spectacular three-to-four hour drive north to the town of Ruhengeri. The lush, dramatic mountains are striped with terraces and patchworked with fields where, among other crops, sorghum, tea, bananas, potatoes and maize grow. Accommodation options in the region are fairly limited, but the most spectacularly located is undoubtedly Virunga Lodge. Perched on a high ridge, it is surrounded by volcanoes and overlooks two vast lakes: Bulera and Ruhondo. Every morning and evening, as the villagers in the valley light their fires, a wispy blanket of smoke extends a further layer of mystery to the enchanting landscape.

An early morning drive to the national park office takes you along very rugged tracks to the village of Kinigi, 15 km north-west of Ruhengeri. Anchored along a ridge of six volcanoes, the Parc National

Members of Susa Group on Karisimbi volcano

Susa Group is the largest in Rwanda

des Volcans is part of a unique conservation initiative that links it with adjoining parks in Uganda and the DRC to create an extensive 650-sq.-km protected habitat for the mountain gorillas. It also became home to Dian Fossey, who fell in love with these animals during a visit in the 1960s and lived among them for about 20 years, conducting ground-breaking studies and protecting them from poachers. The Dian Fossey Gorilla Fund continues her work in the park and a lengthy trek up the Bisoke volcano leads you to her grave – she was mysteriously murdered in 1985.

Park guides explain about gorilla life

Our tracking experience started after another short drive, from the park office up towards the 3634-metre Sabinyo volcano. Soon after leaving our vehicle and the throngs of children and other villagers keen to bid us farewell, we swapped agricultural fields for thick stands of bamboo as we climbed further into the park. Unseen ahead of us, trackers were hunting for the trail the gorillas would have left when they moved on from where they had nested the evening before. We were looking for 13 Group, one of five gorilla groups in the park, which is led by a particularly successful silverback male called Munane. As with any wildlife trip, there are no guarantees – tracking can take

anything from an hour to a day depending on what the gorillas are doing and how fast they are moving.

Seasonal rains had turned the narrow trail into a mess in places, and after slipping and sliding around the first few pools of mud we realized that the best way was the straight way. Ducking and clambering through the bamboo thickets was great fun and the sense of adventure grew the further up the volcano we climbed. Eventually, our trackers appeared ahead. The gorillas, we assumed, were still a little way off.

Leaving our backpacks behind – they could scare the gorillas – we left the main trail and scrambled through dense undergrowth. To our surprise we saw our first gorilla, the immensely powerful-looking Munane, almost immediately, sitting in the grass of a small clearing and staring intently at us. It was an incredible moment, and slightly unnerving too, as we knew he held the only rule book for the encounter. We hardly dared to breathe while the trackers made soothing grunting noises to assure him that we were not out to cause him problems, and he seemed to accept our arrival in his kingdom. In front of him, nursing a curly-haired five-month-old baby, was one of Munane's nine females – an unusually high number of admirers.

All gorilla encounters are limited to one hour, but that hour seemed to last a lifetime as we watched the daily life of 13 Group: the baby intent on eating anything around him, clambering over his mother or simply climbing bamboo shoots until they snapped, sending him tumbling to the forest floor and us into muffled giggles. It was like watching a human family out for a Sunday picnic. As the rains came down again, we slid our way back down the trail and returned to Virunga Lodge to dry out.

Chilling out with Susa Group

Dominant male silverbacks lead the gorilla groups

The following day we went in search of the 40-strong Susa Group – a wonderful trek up the flanks of Rwanda's highest peak, the 4507-metre Karisimbi volcano. The drive there took us through a succession of villages where children played with sticks and hoops while older people carried unfeasible loads of chickens, beer and grass on rickety bicycles. Eventually, the rough four-wheel-drive track petered out and the trek began in earnest, up through steeply terraced fields.

An hour and a half later, the trackers appeared and we scrambled down a steep, overgrown slope to be greeted by the mesmerizing sight of about 20 gorillas in a large, open clearing. In contrast to 13 Group, who had been at rest, Susa, which boasts four silverbacks, nine females and an array of youngsters, was busy feeding and playing. For a magical hour we watched as the young gorillas fought and tumbled while the older ones moved slowly around, crunching their way through bamboo shoot after bamboo shoot. Memorably, the group gave us a momentary glimpse of their new two-week-old baby. Any wildlife encounter brings a sense of wonder, but meeting the gorillas is different. It is like stepping back millions of years to find an ancient mirror reflecting an image not too unlike yourself.

Village in the foothills of Karisimbi volcano

ⓘ ··

Permits to track the gorillas are tightly controlled and are often booked well in advance, so plan ahead. Visitor numbers are strictly limited. There are five gorilla groups, each of which can be tracked by a group of up to eight people each day. Physical contact with the gorillas is strictly forbidden. A significant percentage of the permit fee goes back into conservation and development projects in villages surrounding the park. Several companies, including UK-based Discovery Initiatives, organize full gorilla tours to suit your own itinerary and can arrange accommodation at the lovely Virunga Lodge. Kenya Airways offer the best flight options to Kigali from Nairobi, with connecting international flights.

Yukon river journey
Canada

Stocked up with provisions and paddling onto Lake Laberge

The Yukon River runs through wild, unpopulated country

One of the most famous gold rushes took place in 1897, when the precious metal was discovered in the Klondike. Yet it was far more than just a story of gold and glory. To get to their destination, aspiring miners had to endure a daunting and perilous river journey from Whitehorse to what rapidly became Dawson City. These days, with modern canoe equipment, paddling the same route is one of the best ways to see the raw wilderness of the magnificent Yukon while getting a little taste of what life was like for a Klondike gold rusher.

With 742 km and a week or so of paddling separating Whitehorse from Dawson City, and very limited encounters with civilization en route, this is a trip that must be planned. You need to carry enough food for the entire journey, a barbecue and, of course, seats and a table for dinner in the evening. With expert help from a Whitehorse canoe-outfitter all this, and more, will fit into a standard Canadian canoe – you can even take a cheeseboard.

By the time the original gold rushers reached Whitehorse they had already made an arduous 53-km trek across the mountains on the Chilkoot Trail from Dyea, near Skagway on the Alaskan coast. In the tough winter conditions many people froze to death and others succumbed to exhaustion brought on by transporting huge loads of equipment and belongings. Those who survived the trail were faced with having to build boats at Lake Bennett, to tackle the Yukon River and its notorious rapids. Thankfully, the most dangerous of these, at Miles Canyon, are above the starting point for the modern paddling journey.

The 3700-km-long Yukon flows into the Bering Sea and, along with the Missouri, is the second-longest river in North America – the longest is the Mississippi. In Whitehorse it looks wide and lazy from afar, but up close you'll see that the flow is relentless and rapid. Packed to the gunnels with food and camping gear, the canoe feels heavy and listless when it is first turned into the river. The current carries you swiftly along, then goes slack when the Yukon enters the vast expanse of Lake Laberge.

Rainbow over the river near Camacks

Paddling along the 52-km east shore – preferred by many canoeists as it is 3 km shorter than the opposite one – is a challenge. Catch the lake on a calm day and it is a mirror of tranquillity, especially in the golden evening light. However, when the wind gets up, which may happen without warning, it can turn into a raging sea of white horses with substantial waves. Whatever the weather, it is at least a six-hour paddle to the other end of the lake, more than enough for the first day of the journey.

Before setting up camp alongside the river it is wise to check for bear tracks. There are both black and grizzly bears in the Yukon, and blocking their habitual trails with your tent would not be a good start to your stay in their territory. It is also wise to heed advice about cooking away from your living quarters and storing food either high up in a tree or in airtight barrels. Luckily, your only encounters with these magnificent creatures are likely to be while you are paddling and they are foraging on the river bank.

The most dramatic section of the Yukon, with a swift flow and sharp bends, is known as the Thirty Mile, and is where you will begin to see evidence of the gold-rush heydays: old woodyards and huts that stored the fuel for the paddle steamers that negotiated the rapids to Dawson City once the rush was well under way. It was a journey fraught with danger, and you soon pass the SS *Klondike*, now engulfed by silt, before reaching Hootalinqua island, final resting place of the SS *Evelyn*. This huge disintegrating ship, built in 1908, was abandoned after only one season. Wandering around the hulking wreck, set back from the river at the top of a ramp, gives a striking insight into the expectations – ultimately unfulfilled – that the gold rush must have generated in many of the people who took part in it. Of the hundred thousand people who came seeking their fortunes, only around thirty thousand made it as far as the goldfields. Far fewer struck it lucky.

After Hootalinqua the current becomes more gentle, and you may be fortunate enough to see moose crossing the river, elusive dall sheep with fancy curved horns or bald eagles swooping from their

Loading the canoe at Lake Laberge

SS *Klondike* shipwreck

Shipwreck of the SS *Klondike*, victim of the treacherous rapids

Fort Selkirk is an old trading post

perches high in the trees to take fish from the water. At times the flow is so gentle that you can up your paddles and lie back, enjoying the peace of wilderness life as the canoe drifts downriver. It may come as a rude shock to arrive at Camacks, a small village with one of only four bridges along the Yukon.

The most difficult rapids of the journey await you beyond Camacks, at Five Fingers. The ride through them is bumpy, but once you bob out on the other side you'll soon be back to the gentle, relaxing waters you're used to. From Minto, a good place to stay overnight – one of the campsites is owned by an ex-trapper called Heinz – it is a short paddle to Fort Selkirk. The best-preserved settlers' community on the river, it was established as a trading post in 1848 by Robert Campbell, of the Hudson's Bay Company. It became a major stopping point during the gold rush and even housed a police force. Wandering around its fascinating wooden houses and other buildings gives you a real feel for what life was like at the time.

The final stretch of the journey seems to take a long time, as the river widens and the current becomes even slower, but the wait is well worth it. Dawson City is unique, with its dirt streets, wooden boardwalks and brightly painted, yet slightly dilapidated, wooden houses. You could be excused for thinking you have walked on to the set of a cowboy movie. It was here that many gold rushers ended up, and it still evokes their lawless, hard and fast lifestyle. You can pan for gold, even today, so strike it lucky and you may not want to leave.

ⓘ ···

You can fly to Whitehorse via Vancouver with, among a few other airlines, Air Canada. It is a spectacular flight. Several operators in Whitehorse offer canoe trips on the Yukon, including Kanoe People, who have excellent knowledge of the entire river. You need to take the bear threat seriously and carry pepper spray and bear bangers – small fireworks that create a loud bang – just in case you have an encounter. The best time for paddling is during the summer months, June to September, when there is plenty of daylight and it is warm.

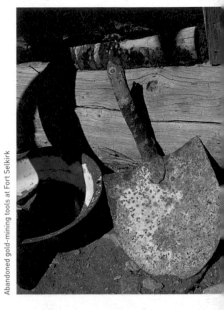

Abandoned gold-mining tools at Fort Selkirk

Gold-panning competition in Dawson City

The bench in Parque Güell

Few geniuses have had the impact on a major city that architect Antonio Gaudí had on Barcelona. His stirring use of colour, shape and form, often inspired by his admiration for nature, are reason enough to visit the great Catalan capital. However, venture just a little further and you can follow the trail of Gaudí's life from Reus, where he was born and went to school, and across the sweeping landscapes of Catalonia, which gave him so much inspiration.

Ceiling roses beneath the square at Parque Güell

Bronze statue of the young Antonio Gaudí in Reus

Born in 1852 in rural Reus, 110 km south-west of Barcelona, Gaudí was the youngest son of an ironmonger and boilermaker. His early life was sculpted by difficulties brought on by rheumatism. Unable to walk far, he was often forced to stay at home, leaving him plenty of time to absorb the elements of nature that surrounded his parents' house.

Today Reus is a busy provincial town, but Gaudí's influence is still felt and honoured there. A short stroll around its pleasant streets takes you to the touching, bronze sculpture of the young Antonio sitting on a bench playing marbles, then past the Iglesia de San Pedro where he was christened and on to the interactive Gaudí museum.

Spiral stairway in La Sagrada Familia

La Sagrada Familia's towers

Tree-like forms inside La Sagrada Familia

Façade de Passion, La Sagrada Familia

Driving through the countryside around Reus you see the natural forms that shaped his thinking. In the rugged and beautiful Pradell mountains to the west, accessed via steep and snaking back roads, tree trunks in open forests echo the support structures that Gaudí used so effectively in his buildings. Indeed, while designing La Sagrada Familia, his iconic cathedral in Barcelona, he said the interior would resemble 'a forest of trees'. Wonky towers of limestone

stand sentinel over the Mediterranean coastal plain and shimmering sea far below, while palm fronds, one of Gaudí's favourite design motifs, fan out from the dry, sun-scorched ground.

As you head back into Barcelona, it is worth making a short detour from the main coast road to see Gaudí's unusual work in the tiny village of Garraf, between Sitges and Castelldefels. Built between 1895 and 1901, the angular Güell Bodegas was used by Eusebi Güell

Curves in the attic at Casa Batlló

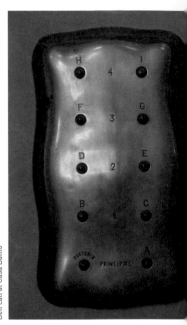

Bell call at Casa Batlló

Sensuous curves in Casa Batlló

to store wine for his export business and features an imposing, iron chain-mail gateway. Another Gaudí masterpiece within easy reach on your return to the city is the remarkable crypt of the church of Colonia Güell at Santa Coloma de Cervelló, which is often regarded as the architect's most pure work.

Deep in the heart of Barcelona, on the Passeig de Grácia, its main thoroughfare, Casa Batlló looks as if it has melted in the intense Spanish sun. Its curvaceous exterior is brought to life by thousands of coloured ceramic tiles and stained-glass windows, balconies shaped like theatrical eye-masks and a roof that looks like an iguana's scaly skin. Inside a seamless flow of curves on swishing staircases and sensuous doors leads you up, around a sky-blue atrium, into the attic area. Here, simple white roof arches tempt you onwards and up, on to that scaly roof where a whimsical collection of chimneys topped with colourful, ceramic balls awaits you.

Not far from Casa Batlló is La Pedrera, also known as Casa Milá, one of Gaudí's final private works in the city. Also built for the Güell family, it is most noted for the unique wave-like forms of its exterior walls and the fantastical Expressionist chimneys and vent structures on its roof.

Of course, no visit to Barcelona or journey into Gaudí's life can ignore La Sagrada Familia, the towering spires of which dominate the skyline and have become the symbol of the city. This was his greatest work, but sadly it wasn't finished in his lifetime – in fact, it has still not been completed and is almost always surrounded by scaffolding. The Façade of the Nativity and the more modern Façade of the Passion alone warrant a few hours of inspection. Inside, among Gaudí's promised forest of trees, a seemingly endless coil of spiral steps takes you to the towers, which afford stunning views of Barcelona.

A window inside Casa Batlló

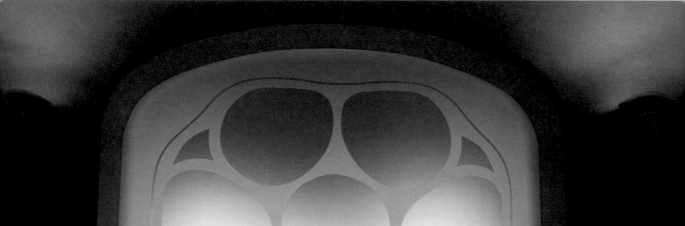

The roof of Casa Batlló

A perfect place to finish your journey through Gaudí's life is the Parque Güell, on a hill in the suburb of Gracia. This beguiling public park boasts an array of his most vibrant work, including the sinuous, mosaic-tiled bench seat on the raised, colonnaded square and candy-coloured, gingerbread-shaped pavilions. This is where the people of Barcelona come to relax and enjoy the sunset, so you might as well join them and bask in the genius that was Antonio Gaudí.

ⓘ ....

If you intend to visit several of Gaudí's buildings buy a Gaudí Route Ticket, which entitles you to discounts off the entry fees. There is no entry fee for the Parque Güell. The main Gaudí attractions get very busy, so be prepared to queue. As usual, it helps to get there as early as possible. You can take a train to Reus from Barcelona, but you will need to hire a car if you want to explore the surrounding countryside.

Central courtyard at La Pedrera

Casa Batlló's wavy façade

Orissan tribal journey
India

Travelling in India is undoubtedly one of life's most intensely colourful experiences, and Orissa is one of the most vibrant of all the country's states, yet relatively few people know of its rich tribal culture. Tucked away in its southern hills are about 60 unique tribes, many of which have little contact with the outside world, and one of the best ways of getting to see any of them involves stepping back in time with a journey in the classic Ambassador car.

Most Orissan tribes live in the Eastern Ghats hills

The iconic Ambassador car

Villagers making their way to market

Situated on the north-eastern coast, Orissa is among India's poorest states and one of the least developed in terms of tourism infrastructure, but it is exactly this that gives a journey to its tribal lands a true sense of travel.

Before heading south from the capital, Bhubaneshwar, don't miss out on making a trip to Konark, 64 km to the south-east, to see its magnificent Sun Temple, Orissa's main tourist attraction. Built in the

The Sun Temple at Konark

13th century, it has a breathtaking façade of sculpted figures, including elephants and erotic dancers, above 24 huge chariot wheels.

The tribal lands are a 10-hour drive south of the capital, and there can be no finer way to travel in India than in an Ambassador car, a continuing reminder of colonial days. Rolling through the countryside past the vast Chilka Lake – a resting ground for hundreds of species of migratory birds – the road eventually turns westwards and begins the climb into the gentle, forested hills of the Eastern Ghats.

Near Taptapani you will start to see the Kandha, the region's largest tribe. Although modern Indian dress has been adopted by many people on the fringes of the area, some women still stroll the streets wearing a small, wrap skirt below and with their upper body covered in swathes of colourful beads. Stacks of bangles decorate their arms, and large gold and pewter rings dangle from their ears and noses; it's impossible not to admire the strength they must have to carry the extra weight.

A highlight of the journey is a visit to the traditional market of the Dongria Kandha in the village of Chatikana, one of the only markets open to outsiders. The Dongria, a subgroup of the Kandha tribe, number around five thousand. They live mainly in the area around the Niyamgiri hills and speak Kuvi. It is a remarkable fact that although all the tribes live relatively close to each other, each speaks a distinct language, demonstrating their isolation.

This isolation means that many tribespeople speedwalk for up to 50 km just to get to their tribal market, then speedwalk home again. Watching them is like watching an Olympic walking race as they skip over the ground, but these 'athletes' happen to carry large baskets of goods – rice, spices and fresh vegetables – on their heads. The women are adorned with fancy beads, bangles, earrings and neck rings, and they move in perfect unison, often in a flowing line. The bangles play an important role in the search for a partner – young

Arriving at Chatikana market

Bondo tribeswomen going to Onukudelli

Early morning chat in the Bondo Hills

Speedwalking helps Bondo women get to market quickly

Villagers can hike 50 km or more to market

Bondo women look spectacular in their neck rings and beads

Dawn over the Eastern Ghats

Bondo women going to Onukudelli market

Erotic sculptures cover Konark's Sun Temple

boys go to the community dormitory and try to force bangles on to the hands of the girls they would like to marry.

From Chatikana, the road snakes through lush valleys towards Machhkund and on to Onukudelli, the market village of the Bondo, in the Bondo Hills. These people are possibly the best known of the Orissan tribes, but they are also the least visited – partly because their fierce independence means they resist almost any outside influence. The men are renowned for their tempers, especially after they have been drinking the locally made *salap* wine. If you are lucky, you may be able to watch the villagers making their way to market – the women rattling their beads and the men carrying bows and arrows.

What you will see on this journey is no 'made for tourism' tribal re-creation. It is the real deal, and this part of Orissa is one of the few places left on the planet where it is possible to see people who have yet to fall for the lure of the modern world. Perhaps, inevitably, they will eventually succumb, but until then the Orissan tribes offer a memorable and adventurous encounter with beautiful, proud and resilient people.

ⓘ ⋯⋯⋯⋯⋯⋯⋯⋯⋯⋯⋯⋯⋯⋯⋯⋯⋯⋯⋯⋯⋯⋯⋯⋯⋯⋯⋯⋯⋯⋯⋯⋯⋯⋯⋯⋯

A handful of tour operators, including Bhubaneshwar-based Dove Tours, offer this special journey around the Orissan tribes, which takes typically 5–12 days. Tourism infrastructure, such as accommodation, in Bhubaneshwar is improving but the hotels available outside the capital are more basic. A good operator will be able to find the best ones to suit your needs. Several domestic airlines offer flights from Delhi to Bhubaneshwar, or you can travel by train, a long but interesting experience.

Many Orissan tribes have little or no outside contact

A tall-ship voyage
Rome to Venice, Italy

Royal Clipper has 42 sails

Rigging anchor points

Take two of Europe's most historic and romantic cities – Rome and Venice – sail from one to the other on the majestic *Royal Clipper*, and you have a delicious recipe for an Italian travel feast lightly spiced with visits to some of Croatia's most beautiful islands.

Although the *Royal Clipper* is luxurious, this tall ship is also very much a working vessel and passengers are encouraged to take an interest or even a small part, if they wish, in its operation. This voyage

Anchored off the port of Cápri at sunset

goes far beyond an ordinary cruise. The ship itself is such a fascinating part of the trip that over the course of the eleven-day journey
you may learn to differentiate between a jigger staysail and a mizzen
upper topgallant.

Designed under the guidance of its Swedish owner, Mikael Krafft,
and brought into service in 2000, the *Royal Clipper* boasts 42 sails
on five masts that tower almost 60 metres above the water line, and
is currently the world's largest working sailing ship. You will catch

your breath when you first see it moored in Rome's main port, Civitavecchia. And stepping aboard and setting out under full sail into the early evening light, with Vangelis' stirring 'Conquest of Paradise' playing on the PA system, will probably have you hankering after the halcyon days of tall-ship exploration.

On board there is a full array of facilities, from upper-deck swimming pools and a piano bar to spa treatments for when you have

Royal Clipper anchored off Ponza

Fishing boats on Ponza

momentarily overdosed on gazing up at the sails and down at the Mediterranean Sea. The first port of call, by the middle of the second day, is the rocky Italian island of Ponza, part of the Pontine group of islands. Tenders take passengers ashore to a sweeping, curved harbour packed full of blue-and-white fishing boats. A short walk up the hilly streets behind Ponza town offers great views over the bay where the ship is anchored.

Back on board, you can enjoy what seems like a never-ending feast as the *Royal Clipper* sails south overnight for Cápri, off the Bay of

Each evening around sunset, the ship sets out under full sail

Houses clinging to the side of Cápri

Naples. A magnet for tourists, the island's limestone cliffs rise majestically out of the sea. On shore, a cable-car ride takes you up to the main town with its array of high-fashion shops – an ideal place for people-watching as Cápri attracts some of Italy's most well-heeled citizens. A range of excursions on offer from the ship means you can cruise around the island and see its towering cliffs and tiny bays and coves up close. In the evening, as on every evening wind conditions

Royal Clipper anchored off Cápri island

allowing, the sight of the *Royal Clipper* leaving under full sail is a spectacle not to be missed – by either the passengers or the local boats that gather to bid it farewell. With Vangelis becoming for ever imprinted on your mind, sailing off into the sunset is an enchanting experience.

After calling at the Aeolian island of Lipari, and its harbour town overlooked by an impressive castle, get ready for some fireworks. During the late evening the ship circles the active volcano of Stromboli. Standing on deck trying to make sure you see every eruption of red lava into the night sky is a real highlight of the voyage.

Early next morning the *Royal Clipper* anchors off Giardini Naxos in Sicily, for a visit to Taormina, the island's most famous resort. The more adventurous can opt for a hike up Mount Etna; at 3323 metres, it is one of the world's highest volcanoes. After a bus journey to its lower

Sulphur deposits on Mount Etna

Mount Etna is one of the world's most active volcanoes

Days at sea can be spent relaxing in the bow netting

Climbing a mast is a must-do part of the trip

flanks you transfer to a special minibus with oversized wheels, to negotiate the long, black volcanic-rock track to the start of the short hike. The barren landscape is occasionally enlivened by patches of yellow sulphur, and walking around one of the subsidiary vents gives you the chance to feel the heat of the volcano literally beneath your feet. Etna has wrought havoc on the surrounding towns and villages sporadically throughout history – the last major eruption was in 1992.

After a day sailing around the bottom of Italy, the ship heads east towards Greece, and to Corfu in the Ionian Sea. Here you can either take a four-wheel-drive tour of the island, or explore Corfu town itself, where the fortress, the narrow streets of its old part and the royal palace are highlights – as is a gentle stroll along the busy waterfront.

From Corfu, the *Royal Clipper* goes north up the Adriatic Sea, along the Croatian coastline. The first port of call is the walled city of Dubrovnik. Compact, and awash with shops, street cafés and historical buildings, it is without a doubt one of the world's most picturesque cities and a delight to explore. Spend an afternoon here and you will be sad to leave. An overnight sail brings you to Korcula, traditionally an island of seafarers. With its tranquil beaches and old town with steep cobbled streets, it makes for an interesting morning ashore. Korcula was on Marco Polo's route to and from Venice, and in an old tower in the town centre there is a small museum about him.

Another short overnight sail leads to the fashionable island of Hvar. Its harbour is lined with an array of super-luxury yachts, so it is no surprise to find that the port gives the impression of being the setting for a fashion show rather than a place for mooring ships. If you can drag yourself away from the action, a reasonable hike takes you to the fort on the overlooking hill. The views, rather than the building itself, are worth the effort. Back in the port there is a 16th-century arsenal and a 17th-century cathedral, Katedrala Sv. Stjepana,

A yacht sailing off Corfu

Sunset is a magical time to be on deck

The beautiful walled city of Dubrovnik

Fortress walls of Hvar

both of which are worth a visit. Most people, though, just seem to want to sit around and watch other people.

Nearing Venice, the *Royal Clipper* calls at the island of Losinj, a nature-lover's paradise. Whether you choose to take a bike ride or explore the forested coastline in one of the ship's kayaks, it makes for a refreshing last encounter with Croatia. Early on the final morning the ship sails into Venice's famous canal system. Most passengers opt to stay in the city for a few days, to soak up the waterway culture and reflect on a classic tall-ship voyage.

ⓘ ⋯⋯⋯⋯⋯⋯⋯⋯⋯⋯⋯⋯⋯⋯⋯⋯⋯⋯⋯⋯⋯⋯⋯⋯⋯⋯⋯⋯⋯⋯⋯⋯⋯⋯⋯⋯⋯

The *Royal Clipper* is part of the Star Clippers fleet of sailing ships and goes from Venice to Rome as well as from Rome to Venice. It also sails in the Caribbean. It is suitable for anyone of just about any age, and you do not have to take part in its operation – a few passengers, but not many more, have a go. Life on board is relaxed and generally informal. It is easy enough to find flights, with scheduled and low-cost airlines flying into Rome and out of Venice, or vice versa, to match your itinerary.

Leaving Hvar under full sail

Venice's Grand Canal

Sunset leaving Losinj

Journey to the Sounds of Wine
Marlborough, New Zealand

Vineyards below Wither Hills, Blenheim

You don't have to be into bungee jumping or *Lord of the Rings* to put New Zealand on your list of dream destinations. Marlborough and Nelson, districts at the northern end of South Island, offer a stunningly beautiful coastline with mountains and countless islands sliced by tranquil, azure inlets, while just inland are some of the world's best wine producers and vineyards. So, pour yourself a Sauvignon Blanc, relax and take a slow-paced Kiwi road trip to remember.

Visitors to New Zealand are spoilt for choice when it comes to breathtaking landscapes, but Marlborough Sounds, which encompasses three sounds along the coast on the Cook Strait between South and North Islands, is outstanding even in such illustrious company. If you want to bookend your drive with visits to wineries,

a good route to take is from Blenheim, in the east and heart of the Marlborough wine region, to Nelson on the west coast, where you can taste the offerings of the Moutere Hills boutique wineries.

There are numerous ways to access Marlborough Sounds, including a ferry ride to Picton from Wellington on North Island. However, if you start your travels from Christchurch, home of South Island's main international airport, you will have the advantage of

Marlborough is famous for its Sauvignon Blanc

Johanneshof is a boutique winery on the road to Picton

travelling up the awesome Pacific Coast Highway, via Kaikoura. Driving along the road as white-roller waves thunder against the rocks spraying it with a fine mist is quite an experience.

Set inland from the sweeping arc of Cloudy Bay, in a broad flat valley that rises to the Wither Hills in the south, Blenheim is about a four-hour drive north of Christchurch and just 25 km south of Picton. Surrounded by more than 70 wineries, and a few hundred additional vineyards that supply the main producers, this pleasant town is a perfect base for sampling the international-award-winning Marlborough wines. Several operators in town offer wine tours, so you don't have to drive and risk getting on the wrong side of the law. For the more energetic, there is always the option of taking a cycling tour of the wineries – as they are concentrated in a compact, flat area, it is a refreshing way to work off any effects between tastings.

Decorative vine canopy at Hunter's Wines, Blenheim

An obvious winery to start at is Montana, with its excellent visitor centre, just out of town on Highway 1 to Kaikoura. It led the way by planting Marlborough's first commercial vines in 1973, and since then has been at the forefront of the rapid rise to fame that New Zealand wines have enjoyed. Although the region produces a wide variety of high-class wines, from Pinot Noir to Riesling, it is the crisp, clean and fruity Sauvignon Blanc that has gained Marlborough its reputation as

Beautiful valley on the way to Portage

Cloudy Bay is the iconic Marlborough winery

one of the world's leading centres of wine production. From here, you can head out along Highway 6 towards Renwick, a small satellite village, to explore the many wineries on the adjoining back roads.

Each winery has its own atmosphere and all are worth visiting but, given limited time or capacity for alcohol, the highlights on the south side of the highway include Wither Hills and Highfields Estate with its Tuscan tower and great views over the valley. If you happen to be here in February, you can take in the Marlborough International Wine Festival, which is held on a dedicated site near Fairhall Downs – another must-see winery. On the north side, don't miss Wairau River; Herzog with its Michelin-rated restaurant, Alan Scott; iconic Cloudy Bay – the most internationally recognized label – and Hunter's. The last is particularly acclaimed and produces superb Sauvignon Blanc.

From Blenheim, it is a short, twisting drive through the hills to Picton; a stop en route at the Johanneshof winery is recommended. The main port for the Interislander ferry to and from North Island,

Picton is at the head of the dramatic Queen Charlotte Sound. A wide range of options is available for exploring the area, from sea kayaking and dolphin-watching to a cruise on the mail boat that delivers post and packages to tiny settlements in remote bays. Hikers can walk along the Queen Charlotte Track, which winds for 72 km from Anakiwa to Ship Cove through the mountains that divide Queen Charlotte Sound from Kenepuru Sound. There are access points for boats, so you can spend anything from a few hours walking part of it to four days hiking the entire trail.

From Picton one of New Zealand's most beautiful drives, the 40-km-long Queen Charlotte Drive, heads west towards Havelock. Offering wonderful views of secluded bays, and taking you through heavily forested hills, the route also provides access, at Linkwater, to a spectacular road that corkscrews along the east shore of

There are several hundred vineyards in Marlborough

Bays dot the Marlborough Sounds, on the road to Portage

Portage is a secluded marina in Queen Charlotte Sound

Kenepuru Sound

Kenepuru Sound – with barely a straight section anywhere along the way, you may feel as though you have been on a fairground ride by the time you reach Portage and its peaceful bay.

Havelock is the greenshell mussel capital of New Zealand, if not the world, and no visit to this town at the head of Pelorus Sound is complete without washing down a huge bowl of mussels with a bottle of Sauvignon Blanc. From here you join Highway 6 and head further west through the foothills of the Richmond Range to the narrow gorge at Pelorus Bridge, and onwards into the picturesque Rai Valley. Another twisting road detours north towards French Pass, taking you through the village of Okiwi Bay, which is set dramatically in the snug, mountainous cove of Croisilles Harbour.

Back on the main route, it is not long before you reach the waters of Tasman Bay and the city of Nelson. While there is plenty to see here, wine buffs will want to continue south for a short distance, to Motueka. Set on the open Waimea Plains, a clutch of superb boutique wineries nestles in the gentle slopes of the adjoining Moutere Hills.

Previous pages: Late afternoon sunshine over Havelock, famed for its greenshell mussels   Rimu Grove winery in Upper Moutere, Nelson

Sunset at Havelock

Okiwi Bay on the road to French Pass

If you are loath to leave the wine behind, they will deliver – so you will be able to enjoy the Kiwi dream life long after you return home.

ⓘ ··

It is easy to access the Marlborough region from either Christchurch, on South Island, or Wellington, on North Island, via the Interislander ferry. Car rental is available at the cities' airports. Be careful to check the insurance excess as this can be quite substantial – you can reduce but not eliminate it by paying an extra charge per day. New Zealand's roads are generally quiet and make for excellent driving. However, the going can be quite slow because of the number of curves, so don't underestimate the driving time. A wide range of good-value accommodation is available throughout the area.

Havelock is the main port for greenshell mussels

Sea kayaking cays
The Exumas, the Bahamas

Exploring Stocking Island

Surrounded by dazzling azure seas and lined with secluded, pristine-white beaches, hidden coves and isolated bays, the 160-km-long Exumas island chain is a Caribbean cocktail not to be missed. Here the warm breezes of the trade winds, the world's clearest waters and 365 different coral island cays create a sea paddler's paradise.

Only 56 km south-east of Nassau, the Exumas lie in the heart of the 259,000-sq.-km Bahamas archipelago. And a sea kayak is the very best way to explore them. These stable boats provide the perfect vantage point, allowing you to serenely glide above the crystal waters, floating over an ever-changing underwater world

The word 'Bahamas' comes from the Spanish *baja mar* (shallow sea) and this lack of depth prevents cruising yachts and larger vessels from penetrating too close to land, which means you can slip

Kayaks at Rat Cay

almost silently from bay to bay accompanied only by the gentle sounds of your kayak paddle dipping in and out of the water. Such is the clarity of the sea, you can spot anything from manta rays to nurse sharks from your cockpit.

With special storage hatches in the kayak to carry your camping equipment and food, your journey will take you well and truly away from the hustle and bustle of modern life into this lesser-known and undeveloped part of the Bahamas. Here palm-fringed bays, coconut palms and occasional conch shells give your evening campsite a distinctly castaway feel. Sitting on a secluded beach and looking out on a vast ocean, as the sun dips off the edge of the horizon and sets the sky ablaze in a storm of vibrant oranges and reds, will certainly provide a taste of the tropical magic of the Caribbean.

The largest single land mass in this chain of islands is Great

New Cay

Landing at Lily Cay

Exuma to the south. The main airstrip, and therefore the main gateway for visitors, is a 30-minute drive from George Town, the island's administrative centre. Located on the west shore of Elizabeth Harbour and sheltered from the Atlantic by lagoon-laced Stocking Island, the town is bisected by the tropic of Cancer. In the shelter of its attractive bay, where the annual Family Island Regatta is held, you can get to grips with your kayak before venturing further afield.

At the northern end of Great Exuma, 40 minutes' drive from George Town, the sleepy village of Barretarre provides a natural starting point for the journey. From here you can easily access the outer windward cays of Exuma Sound, including Boysie Cay and Rat Cay and the sheltered Brigantine chain – a thin stretch of remote islands to the west which, seen from the air, almost seem to be linked like

Exploring mangroves, Long Cay

stepping stones. Island hopping from cay to cay in your kayak takes you through a variety of waters, ever-changing in their appearance.

Boysie Cay is a short distance away – ideal for a first-day paddle – and provides you with a camping spot on a sandy spit. From here a hollowing in the rocks on the north-east side of the island gives a view on to the deeper waters of the Atlantic. When the swell is running it's a good place for watching waves.

At the most northerly tip of Great Exuma, where you round Pudding Point, the water changes once again. The seabed rarely disappears from sight and when the light is bright the rich aquamarines of the peaceful undisturbed sea glisten against a skyline of dazzling cornflower blues.

Further along the Brigantine chain, as you pass isolated coves, secret hidden bays, and islands with names like Gold Ring Cay, False Cay and Jimmy Cay, the route conjures up a sense of the past when pirates sailed the waters and raided boats that were lured into the shallows. On the southern tip of Long Cay, a sweeping palm-backed

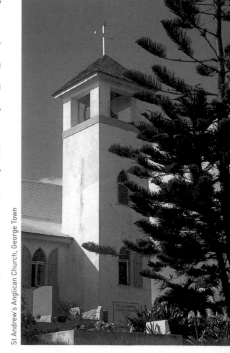

St Andrew's Anglican Church, George Town

Mangroves in the morning light, Long Cay

Morning skies, Long Cay

bay is an obvious stopping point and provides the opportunity for you to do some plundering of your own by quenching your kayaking thirst with freshly fallen coconuts.

When you reach New Cay you will easily be able to follow its rocky limestone shoreline into the inner lagoon at the south-east end of the island. This leads to Mangrove Creek, which can be navigated at high tide when the lush greens and twisted roots of the mangroves provide yet another vibrant colour contrast.

For your return journey to Great Exuma you could simply reverse the route and paddle along the opposite side of the chain. Or you could kayak north-east across the Brigantine Bank and aim for Norman's Pond Cay, then island hop from Lee Stocking Island to Williams Cay and Children's Bay Cay before reaching a pretty bay and your final camping spot on Rat Cay.

This paddle to and from Great Exuma is just one option. The many islands, and the protected and secluded waters, mean you are spoilt for choice as to where to explore. An alternative journey could start

A sunset paddle, Long Cay

on Little Exuma, the northernmost part of the chain. Between Wax Cay Cut and Conch Cay Cut you can kayak through the Exumas Land and Sea Park, the world's first replenishment nursery. Established in 1958 as a no-take fishery reserve it is famous for its pristine beauty, outstanding anchorages and breathtaking marine environment. Here it's possible to share your campsite with 200-year-old tortoises, sea turtles and even the Bahamian dragon – a type of iguana.

No route need be the same. With easy waters to navigate and the ever-changing light and colours you may just wish you could be shipwrecked and stay a little longer on these tropical paradise islands.

ⓘ ....

Kayaking tours are run by Starfish, the only Exumas-based kayak operator. From George Town they run day trips as well as multi-day tours and also provide fully catered trips with a support boat. Their Classic Exuma Kayak ten-day trip includes four days and three nights of kayak touring, staying on isolated beaches on the islands north of Great Exuma. The last three nights are spent in comfortable lodgings in or near George Town, giving you the opportunity to sail, dive, bike or take an Eco-boat tour.

Slicing its way through the steep, ragged mountains of the Sierra Madre range in north-west Mexico, Copper Canyon is home to one of the world's most dramatic rail journeys. Within 653 km, the Chepe train takes you on a breathtaking ride to a height of over 4000 metres and back to sea level – across the great plains of Chihuahua, through the mountains and across the Pacific coastal plain to Los Mochis.

Opposite: Winding into the foothills of the Sierra Madre from Chihuahua

Chepe train engine

This is not a trip where you simply sit and gawp out of the window. There is plenty to see and do en route, from visiting traditional Mexican towns and Tarahumara Indian villages to hiking through a canyon, so most travellers break up the 15-hour journey by spending a night or two at stops along the line. With only one first class, or 'tourist', train a day – the Chepe Primera Express – running in each direction any break entails an overnight stay. The first class train benefits from smartly uniformed guards, air-conditioned carriages and seat space to rival flying business class, so you really can relax.

123

The Chepe leaves the town of Chihuahua in the murky light of dawn, and doesn't take long to exit it and enter the open grassy plains – an opportunity for majestic sunrise watching. As the heat of the day rapidly vanquishes the night chill the train speeds along the often arrow-straight line. From it you get a snapshot of daily Mexican life unaffected by your presence. Alongside the track young and old men, most of them wearing cream-coloured panama hats, head off to work on foot or by bicycle. A little later, passing through small towns like Santa Isabel and San Andrés, scores of children in neat crisp uniforms can be seen walking eagerly to school.

Open country near Chihuahua

Beyond the first main stop, the town of Cuauhtémoc, the line passes through thousands of hectares of apple orchards grown by the large population of Mennonites who came to the region in the early 1920s. Their beliefs are based on 16th-century Anabaptist teachings with an emphasis on community, and some of the older order still lead a traditional existence, rather like the Amish, without electricity or cars. Some 50 km further on, at La Junta, the train begins its inexorable journey up into the Sierra Madre mountains, travelling alongside small rivers and traversing beautiful, lush valleys. The windows in the doors between the carriages are the only ones that open, and offer the best views of the dramatic landscape. The temperature will begin to cool noticeably, though, as the train gains height.

Even now, with the most spectacular parts of the journey still to come, what has been achieved by building the railway line in such a wild and unforgiving environment is something to marvel at. The track bends and twists upwards like a serpent, passing through cuttings hewn from the rock and, in its entire length, crossing no fewer than 36 bridges and going through 87 tunnels. Completed in 1961, after

Divisadero is perched on the edge of Copper Canyon

Copper Canyon, the world's largest canyon system

Bridge at Témoris

almost 90 years of on-and-off construction, it is widely recognized as one of the world's greatest feats of engineering.

Many travellers opt to spend a night at the next stop, the sawmill town of Creel, which is a good base for tours into Copper Canyon and out to surrounding Tarahumara villages. However, if you want to stay somewhere very special it is worth remaining on board for the next 50 km until the train reaches Divisadero, a tiny, one-hotel village perched on the very edge of the canyon. The Chepe routinely stops here for 15 minutes so that passengers can take photographs. It is a pity to rush through, though, especially as you arrive in Divisadero around midday when the light bleaches the canyon, making it look less impressive. An overnight stop also means that you get to stay in one of the world's most spectacularly located hotels, where the best rooms have balconies literally on the canyon edge, giving spectacular views of the sunset and sunrise.

Divisadero is a good spot for a guided hike along the rim of the canyon or, for those with a few days to spare, an extended hike to the bottom, which involves camping en route. There, the alpine terrain of the upper canyon is replaced with a tropical landscape where mango and orange trees grow. Copper Canyon is in fact a commonly used term that refers to an interconnecting network of six canyons. Together they cover an area four times larger than the USA's Grand Canyon. They go much deeper too, with the deepest – Urique Canyon – plunging 1879 metres from the rim.

Another good reason to stop overnight in Divisadero is that you can board the train again refreshed for the most spectacular part of the journey. The line plummets through incredible tunnels and switchbacks as the steep canyon walls and rugged peaks soar high above. At times it seems to defy gravity as it clings to a cliff face on one side with, on the other, a sheer drop to a turbulent river. At Témoris

Crossing the plains near Creel

Narrow tunnel above Témoris

it performs a virtuoso triple switchback, during which you can see all three levels, that will leave you amazed at how far the line has dropped towards the valley floor. With a waterfall cascading into the Septentrión River and monolithic rock pinnacles thrusting from the river bed, Témoris is one of the jewels in the Copper Canyon crown.

The landscape continues to enthral as the line winds its way towards El Descanso and Loreto, crossing tall river bridges and skirting beautiful lakes. Eventually, the terrain relents, the temperature increases and the train returns to its higher speeds as it heads west over the coastal plain to El Fuerte. A few hours further on, Los Mochis is the official end of the line. However, as this town is rather characterless,

Previous pages: Hiking trails from Divisadero offer great views of Copper Canyon   Lake scenery near Loreto

many people choose to end their journey at colonial El Fuerte. Sitting in its resplendent plaza lined with palm trees, enjoying the warm evening air, you will be able to reflect on the train ride of a lifetime.

ⓘ ···

The Chepe first class train runs once a day in each direction all year round. The second class train, used mainly by locals, also operates once a day but is slower and offers none of the comforts of the first class one. Tickets can be bought with as many stopovers as you require, and the journey is very reasonably priced. Although you can buy tickets on the day it is better to reserve them in advance, especially during the busier period of May to October. There are excellent hotels in Chihuahua, Divisadero, Posada de Barrancas and El Fuerte. Other stops may not offer accommodation in the higher range. Both Chihuahua and Los Mochis have airports; flights to the former are usually more competitively priced.

Cutting through the Sierra Madre at Divisadero

Sunset on the plains near Creel

Horse-drawn caravan
Wicklow, Ireland

Beautiful upper lake at Glendalough

If you fancy life in the slow lane, jump aboard a horse-drawn caravan and explore the sleepy country byways and highways of Wicklow in Ireland. It will be just you, an Irish carthorse and the lure of the open road.

This delightfully simple, back-to-basics journey takes you through idyllic pastoral scenes where the barking of farm dogs and the cries of shinty players mid-match mingle with the hum of tractors at work. With your home for the week towed behind you, courtesy of your sturdy horse, you will have the flexibility to go wherever you wish.

Head west and you will discover heather-clad rolling mountains and sharply hewn valleys, including the dramatic Glenmalure, the

longest glacial valley in the British Isles, and Glendalough, with its stunning lakes. To the east you can find a very different landscape of broad, empty beaches backed by tumbling dunes. The road ahead is yours to explore, with the freedom to make up your own itinerary and schedule as you go along.

One of the advantages of this area is that an intricate network of quiet country lanes is immediately open to you, which makes it easy to plan your route. On a few occasions you may need to stray on to busier roads, but these are well marked on the maps you will be given and are not difficult to negotiate.

There are no fixed itineraries as such, but there are a number of

On the trail at Glendalough

recognized overnight spots that have facilities such as showers as well as grazing and water for horses. Most caravanners simply decide on a route that takes them to these spots along the quietest roads.

Caravan country is less than a two-hour drive south of Dublin in the county of Wicklow, also known as the 'garden of Ireland' for its green lushness. But the joys of the open road can be savoured only after a crash course in carthorse management. You will find that having a horse of your own for a week is rather like suddenly gaining a child – an unusually big and hungry one. It becomes the centre of attention and the focus for the start of the day.

At the base at Carrigmore, where you collect the caravan and horse, you will learn all you need to know about your equine friend, including the art of enticing it from its paddock – something you have to do each morning. The secret is to carry a large bucket of oats, which horses are very quick to sniff out and remarkably deft at getting their noses very firmly and quickly planted inside. They then become much more obliging. After the feed you will need to have your hoof pick at the ready to clear the horse's feet of any stones that could make it lame, and will have to brush down its coat and mane.

The job isn't finished when you have caught and cleaned your steed. Next comes fixing the bridle, saddling up and attaching the shafts from the brightly coloured Romany-style caravan so that the horse can pull it. Controlling a half-ton animal can seem daunting to start with, but everything is geared towards helping people who have no previous experience of horses.

Before you know it you are swinging out from the farm gates and on to your first stretch of road, listening to the steady rumble and creak of the wooden caravan and the clipped rise and fall of hoof beats.

Perched on the wooden seat in front of your caravan, reins in hand and with seven days stretching ahead, you can explore the

Forest trail near Glendalough

hedgerow lanes leading from Carrigmore, and slowly go north through the lush green fields surrounding Glenealy and around the foot of Carrick Mountain, to Garryduff and O'Byrne's farm. Here home-made scones and traditional brown bread provide a delicious end to the day.

As you move westwards the landscape steadily begins to change, from leafy hedgerows that in places have grown almost into full arches to more open and mountainous scenery. Glenmalure – a dramatic glacial valley with jagged cliffs at its upper reaches, tumbling waterfalls and dense, fern-covered slopes – offers the very best of this. It's not hard to see why Michael Dwyer, rebel and local folk hero, made this glen a hideout when he was attempting to escape capture by the English army following the rebellion of 1798. Its steep sides, rocky outcrops and thick forests would have provided the perfect cover.

When you head towards the bustling seaside town of Arklow, nestled on the edge of St George's Channel, the scenery is different again: quiet coastal roads provide open views out to sea and lead to the stunning, uncluttered beaches of Brittas Bay to the north.

Fitzgerald's pub in Avoca, which appeared in the BBC TV series *Ballykissangel*

Arriving at Glenmalure

On the road to Garryduff

The slowed-down pace of the caravan, with its steady rhythm, allows you to sit back and take in each new view that comes with every twist in the road. With speed limited to about 6 km an hour you won't be going anywhere fast, so there's plenty of time to soak in the scenery. It's an altogether relaxed, unfussy way of life.

At the end of your journey you will feel that you have covered a lot of ground in only seven days; and find it hard to believe that you have seen so much of the landscape – given just how slowly the horse plods along. You may even feel that a week is not long enough – that the Romany in you has been stirred and the open road ahead is calling.

Dawn near Glenmalure

ⓘ

Clissmann Horse Caravans have been providing self-drive tours since the 1960s and rent four-berth horse-drawn caravans with cooking and sleeping facilities for a week or more. They give full tuition in horse handling and have an established network of farms, hotels and pubs with fields for grazing and overnight parking for caravans. Several international airlines fly to Dublin, and Irish Ferries provide a regular daily service to the city from Holyhead, Wales.

Into the ice bear kingdom

Churchill, Canada

Hudson Bay begins to freeze around November

Every winter in the far northern reaches of Manitoba, at Churchill on the shores of Hudson Bay, polar bears gather to wait for the water to freeze over so that they can hunt seals. Exploring their kingdom aboard an oversized buggy is a remarkable journey into the wild and beautiful tundra at the edge of the Arctic. The reward can be moving, and at times hilarious, encounters with these playful yet deadly bundles of white fur.

Many places in the world are deemed remote, but then you find towns like Churchill. No road has ever made it there, so the only ways in are either to fly – a 2½-hour flight on an old twin-propeller plane – or to go by rail, which takes at least 36 hours. Both plane and train depart from Winnipeg. Whichever way you travel, arriving in the town will

Churchill's main street

initially shock your system. The window of opportunity to see the bears gathering opens in early October and closes in mid-November, lasting around six weeks, which means it is cold, very cold. Not as cold as it gets in January, but chilly enough to make chunky jackets and windproof clothing essential.

At first glance, the simple and unpretentious town – first established in 1717 as a trading post by the Hudson's Bay Company – seems windswept and forsaken. But a short exploration of your surroundings takes you past the ice-covered roads, snow-laden houses and endless surrounding tundra to its Inuit culture, and the warm and hardy people who have made it their home. There are three things that Churchill has in abundance: polar bears – it is tagged the 'polar bear capital of the world' – unrestricted views, and people with

Sunset over the tundra

Sunrise drive to the bear station

Sunset on log house, Churchill

characters big enough to fill a stadium. It seems everyone from your bus driver to restaurant staff has a fully loaded clip of quips ready to fire off on the briefest of encounters. The longer you stay, the more the town, the people and its remarkable landscape get under your skin, and its isolation soon becomes its real appeal.

With only a few other distractions, namely a bar, a sprinkling of restaurants and, if you are lucky, the spectacular aerial shows of the ethereal Northern Lights, the quest to see the polar bears is the main attraction. In the sharp air of early morning, as the sun rises along Kelsey Boulevard, Churchill's main drag, you board a classic old school bus. About half an hour out of town, along the edge of Hudson Bay, you reach the station for the unique tundra buggies. These monster machines are the brainchild of a local guide – they are manufactured in Churchill – and feature tyres big enough to 'float' on top of the soft tundra soil. They may seem over-the-top in the natural wilderness that surrounds you, but as you plunge into the first icy puddle you soon realize that they are the only way to get around such inhospitable terrain. Their impact is limited to an established network of tracks, most of which were made by American tanks: Churchill was a strategic armed forces base from the Second World War to the mid-1980s.

As with most wildlife-focused journeys patience is a prerequisite, but scanning the brown-and-white landscape for any signs of life keeps boredom at bay as the tundra buggy slowly winds its way out towards Gordon Point and further east to Watson Point. In addition to polar bears, you may see other unique northern inhabitants, including caribou, Arctic hares, Arctic foxes, snowy owls and ptarmigans. It is a thrill to see any kind of wildlife, but the first sighting of a polar bear always has the buggy's passengers in raptures. The expert eyes of a naturalist like David Hatch will be a help, as resting bears do excellent imitations of boulders and shrubby mounds when the ground is not entirely covered with snow.

They rarely seem to rest for long, though. They love to play-fight, and if you stop and wait a while you will see them sizing each other up, wrestling and even standing on their back legs – tall and proud like world championship boxers – trading blows and slaps. With male bears weighing in at around 500–600 kg, they are definitely in the heavyweight division, but it is rare for them to inflict any serious injury on each other during these sparring sessions. Females can sometimes be seen escorting their cubs as they pad across one of the

thousands of small, shallow lakes that cover the tundra. The bears' extremely large paws, with exposed black pads and lengthy claws, help to spread their load on thin ice.

As Hudson Bay starts to freeze, which can happen in a matter of days with temperatures of −20°C or below, the bears begin to edge their way out on to the vast expanse of ice in search of seals, their favourite meal. They travel long distances alone and move with the seasonal ebb and flow of the ice looking for tell-tale breathing holes where seals intermittently surface. There they lie, waiting in ambush.

Young males play-fighting

Bears wait patiently for the bay to freeze

Male bears often stand to fight

After driving around the tundra over the course of a few days – the hardy can even stay in special tundra 'motels' made of buggy trailers – you will realize that what at first appeared to be a relatively lifeless, uninhabitable wasteland is in fact awash with life and beauty.

ⓘ ··

Several companies, including Discover the World, organize trips to Churchill to explore the land of the polar bears. Demand is high, and the short season and limited buggy permits mean that booking well in advance is recommended. Hudson Bay Helicopters is one of the companies that offers thrilling flights over the bay area that give wonderful overviews of the tundra and a different way to see the bears and other wildlife. Accommodation options in Churchill are limited, with the Churchill Motel being one of the best. Temperatures can drop severely at any time, and the wind chill can make it feel even colder, so take plenty of warm clothing.

A Bohemian journey
Prague, Czech Republic

Bridges over the Vltava River

Cultured, mystical and awash with beautiful architecture, Prague, the capital of the Czech Republic and one of Europe's most stunning cities, has for centuries been a spiritual home to musicians, poets and artists. It was also the capital of Bohemia, and walking or taking a tram ride through its streets will lead you along routes that Bohemian kings used for their processions. Because Prague is relatively compact, it is possible to enjoy it over a long weekend.

Set majestically astride the Vltava River, Prague is made up of five distinct districts, each with its own character and history. It seems natural to begin your journey in Hradcany, one of the oldest parts of

Café in the Josefov district, the Jewish Quarter

the city, where Prague Castle and its cathedral dominate the hilltop skyline. It is quite a walk to reach the castle, and the best idea is to go up the steps leading from Thunovska street and leave the longer set of steps for your descent to Chotkova street. Both routes are lined with the usual array of souvenir sellers, but there are also artists whose original watercolours and photographs are well worth perusing.

A castle was first built here in the 9th century, during the Premyslid dynasty of Prince Boleslav, and the structure has evolved and been supplemented ever since. The main entrance is off Hradcany Square, where you may find jazz and classical musicians busking near the archbishop's palace. Before entering the castle take

View over Prague from Hradcany

Golden Lane

a peek over the wall alongside the road for a breathtaking view over the red-tiled roofs of the city to the river far below – it's the least you deserve after climbing all those steps.

Once inside the castle, two grand outer courtyards lead into the central one, which is almost overwhelmed by the soaring Gothic façade of St Vitus Cathedral. Constructed initially under the orders of Charles IV in the 14th century, it only reached completion around 600 years later, in 1929. On your way down to Chotkova street, quaint Golden Lane is not to be missed, partly for its delightful coloured and crooked cottages, and also because a visit to number 22, once home to the city's favourite writer and world-renowned author, Franz Kafka, is a must. Kafka's influence still permeates Prague and you could dedicate a few days to finding his old haunts.

Back alongside the Vltava, the Malá Strana district awaits your exploration. It underwent major reconstruction after a fire in 1541, and the Baroque buildings that replaced the ones that were destroyed remain pretty much in their original state. Impressive glass-fronted, pastel-coloured house façades surround the main square, the Malostranské náměstí, which boasts the green-domed St Nicholas Church on its western side. A wide cobbled road in front of the church is divided by a tramline: route 22. If you want to see a quick cross section of the city, a ride along this line, aboard one of Prague's iconic red-and-cream trams, will take you through it.

It is now time to cross the river and, while there are numerous bridges, there is only one that attracts the crowds: Karlov most (Charles Bridge). It is the treasured link that brings both sides of the city together and was part of the procession route used by Bohemian kings. As you stroll down narrow Mostecká street and pass through a forbidding, blackened stone archway on to the bridge, you will find yourself slowing your pace. Charles Bridge was not designed for rushing across. Its solid Gothic walls and cobbled pavements are lined with thirty statues, primarily of saints. Although St Wenceslas is among

Skyline of Malá Strana

Statues line Karlov most (Charles Bridge)

St Vitus Cathedral dominates the Hradcany skyline

Houses along Karlova street

them, the most popular one is that of John of Nepomuk, Prague's vicar-general in the 14th century. He was tossed off the bridge by Wenceslas IV for conspiring against him, and the ring of seven stars around the statue's head represents the seven stars that are said to have glistened on the water where he drowned. The brass relief at the base of the statue, depicting his death, has been rubbed clean by visitors – touching it is meant to ensure you will return to Prague.

When you leave the bridge Karlova street, a narrow twist of cafés and jewellery shops, takes you into the heart of the Staré Mesto (Old Town). At its centre is one of Europe's most impressive public spaces: the Staromestské námestí (Old Town Square). The spires of elegant

City tours can be taken in antique cars

Ornate window decoration in Karlova street

Tram on route 22

Tyn Church preside over the main plaza, but it is the old town hall opposite that attracts all the attention. On its south façade is a fanciful astronomical clock, similar to a complex sundial, and every hour, on the hour, it seems that all of Prague gathers to watch it chime. The figure of Death emerges on the upper portion and sounds the death knell, which sparks a procession of other characters, including Greed, Vanity and the twelve apostles. To continue in the footsteps of the Bohemian kings, follow Celetna street, with its delightful pastel-shaded houses, towards the looming, Gothic powder tower.

In the evening you will be spoilt for entertainment choice, especially if you like classical music. Music runs deep through the veins of Prague

Early morning on Karlov most (Charles Bridge)

Old Jewish cemetery, Josefov district

Houses on the banks of the Vltava

St Vitus Cathedral inside Prague Castle

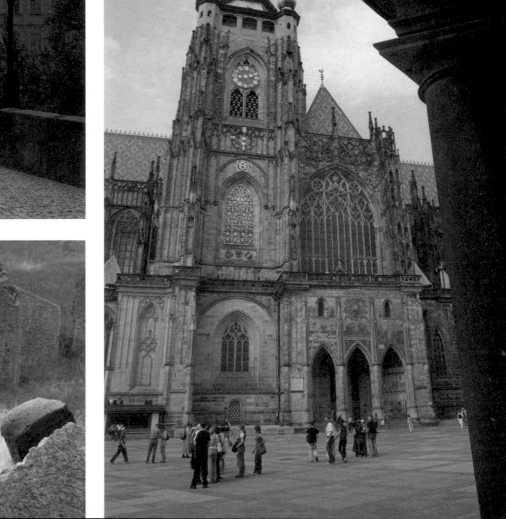

and some of the world's most famous composers visited the city, including Dvorák and Mozart, who premiered *Don Giovanni* here. Every night, the classics are performed in venues around the city.

Josefov (the Jewish Quarter) lies wholly within the Old Town. Noticeably more wealthy than other parts of the city, it is also home to the most moving place in Prague. The old Jewish cemetery is a tumble of gravestones as Jews were buried several bodies deep because of the lack of space afforded them by their persecutors. It is a powerful reminder of the diversity of cultures that has made Prague such a fascinating city to explore.

ⓘ ⋯⋯⋯⋯⋯⋯⋯⋯⋯⋯⋯⋯⋯⋯⋯⋯⋯⋯⋯⋯⋯

Many airlines, including Thomsonfly, offer regular flights to Prague. Although there is plenty of accommodation in the city it can get heavily booked, especially during the summer months of July and August. Hotel Club will book any accommodation you require. If the weather allows, hot-air balloon flights over the outskirts of the city and nearby castles are available. Choose carefully if you want to go to a concert – the standards of performance vary greatly from one venue to another. Don't miss a stroll up the immense, 1-km-long Wenceslas Square in the Nové Mesto (New Town).

Municipal House in Republic Square

Horse-drawn carriages offer city tours

Costa Rica has no rival in Central America when it comes to nature at its most spectacular. It has it in abundance, from raging white-water rivers and active volcanoes to species-rich rainforests and glorious beaches. And there is no better way to explore the country than by using your own power to paddle and pedal along the Pacuare River and through the Nicoya Peninsula – with a little motorized help along the way.

Rafting the Pacuare River

Over eight days, you will get to go rafting, mountain biking, trekking and even sea kayaking as you enjoy the best of what Costa Rica has to offer. Don't despair if you are not a professional athlete. Though you need to be reasonably fit, vehicle back-up on many sections allows you to take a break if the going gets too tough.

Your adventure begins with a two-day, 29-km rafting trip to Siquirres along the beautiful Pacuare with its world-class rapids and true wilderness feel. Flowing from the high peaks of the Cordillera Central, the river's waters head through the valley and eventually reach the Caribbean Sea. The journey involves exciting paddling over

Instruction is given before you start paddling

Grades three-to-four rapids on the Pacuare River

Coffee plantations on the way to Arenal

a series of rapids – classified as grades three to four, they are easily big enough to get you wet and your heart pumping – interspersed with sections of calm water where you can chill out and relax, and which are ideal for wildlife spotting.

The raft put-in point is at Tres Equis near the Turrialba volcano, a 2½-hour drive from Costa Rica's capital, San José. Here, after a comprehensive practice and safety instruction session, you set off down river. Any notion of a quiet introduction to the trip is shattered when the first three rapids are tackled. Paddle 'high fives' are the order of the day as confidence grows with each new onslaught of white, cold water. The best views are from the front of the raft – it just happens that they are of walls of frothy waves heading your way.

The guide steers and barks out paddling commands, and it gets even more thrilling as rapids with ominous names like Landslide and Bumper Rock toss and turn the raft. By mid-afternoon, the sight of your comfortable overnight campsite, El Nido del Tigre (the Tiger's Nest) is very welcome. Nestled in the rainforest, it is a wonderful place for lying in a hammock and watching birds and butterflies flitting in and out of plants and trees.

The second day on the river sees the biggest rapids, several of which feature large boulders halfway through. The key to negotiating them successfully is to listen intently, above the roar of the water, to the guide's commands. It is wise to assume that 'Paddle Forward Hard!' means exactly that – and that it means do it quickly. Without the power of the paddlers, the raft is very hard to steer. If you avoid flipping it, which inevitably leads to a chilly and eventful swim for everyone, it counts as a good run. By the time you arrive at Siquirres you will be proud of your achievement.

A drive north takes you to the perfectly shaped Arenal volcano, one of the most active in the world. If you want to stretch your legs

Mangroves at Tabacón Hot Springs

Biking to the Pacific Ocean, Nicoya Peninsula

Tabacón Hot Springs

after all the paddling, there are several hiking trails on nearby peaks, including Cerro Chato – another volcano. Tackling one of them will give you a good excuse to head for an evening at the luxurious Tabacón Hot Springs resort at the base of Arenal. Here you will be able to relax in beautifully landscaped gardens and thermal pools, and watch as the volcano erupts and red-hot lava flows from the rim of its crater.

Back on the road, you drive for several hours through hills to the Pacific coast, where you saddle up on a mountain bike for a ride down the Nicoya Peninsula to Samara. This takes you through one of the most remote parts of Costa Rica, with long, idyllic beaches that are magical places for pedalling. You also do a little sea kayaking – a perfect way to explore the nooks and crannies of the coastline – before getting back on your bike for a challenging ride south to Malpais.

Beach biking on Nicoya Peninsula

The route diverts inland at times, along quiet, dirt tracks and across wide rivers where you hoist your bike above your head and wade – welcome, cooling relief if the day is hot and humid. The final pedalling section of the journey is along wilderness beaches, including Playa San Miguel. If you are lucky, you may see turtles coming ashore at night to lay their eggs.

Going around Costa Rica under your own steam is richly rewarding; but by the time you see the support bus at the finish line of this superb, at times challenging, journey, the idea of sitting down and doing nothing for a few hours as you head back to San José will be distinctly appealing.

Sea kayaking near Samara

Dawn over the beach at Samara

San José-based Coast to Coast Adventures offers this multisport itinerary for seeing Costa Rica. Equipment is either included or can be hired from them. Some people like to take their own mountain bikes, but good ones can be hired from Coast to Coast. Some of the Pacific beaches are susceptible to strong rip tides, so check with your guide before swimming in the sea. It is important to check with your doctor if you have any condition that can be affected by sustained physical exercise – the heat and humidity can make the journey tough.

Sunset, Nicoya Peninsula

Through Patagonian fjords
Puerto Montt, Chile

Take a cruise through the thousands of wild and desolate islands in the Chonos archipelago along the southern shores of Chile, and you will be more likely to see whales, dolphins and distant icebergs than other ships. And the best thing is you don't have to spend a fortune, as this four-day voyage is one of the planet's great travel bargains.

First up, this is no normal cruise. Until the mid-1990s the journey aboard the ship from Puerto Montt to Puerto Natales, deep in Chilean Patagonia, was the preserve of truck drivers who wanted to avoid the 1450-km haul south on roads of dubious quality, and of a few in-the-know travellers willing to rough it in order to glimpse one of the

The wild and wonderful Last Hope Sound, Puerto Natales

There is a fun atmosphere aboard ship

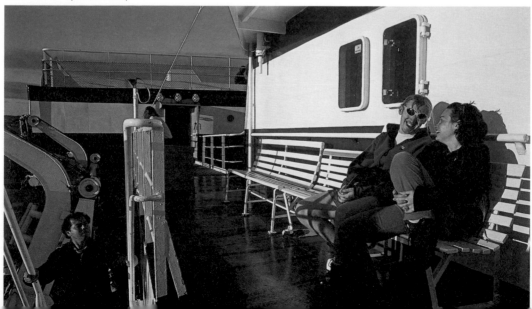

161

planet's least explored areas en route to trekking in the Torres del Paine national park. As word of this amazing voyage spread, the number of travellers increased until the owners of the ship, Navimag, decided to bolt on an accommodation section so that passengers could sleep in comfort. You get three meals a day, can carry on board as much Chilean wine as your backpack can handle – and will revel in the special camaraderie and party spirit that only a four-day cruise on a wine-packed ship can create. And the truck drivers go along too. It's pretty basic, but it's also fabulous fun.

Setting sail in the glowing evening light, the ship soon leaves behind the colourful wooden houses of Puerto Montt and glides through the Ancud Gulf past Chiloé Island – one of Darwin's stop-off points on HMS *Beagle*. On the mainland the striking shapes of two

Threading the boat through the Angostura Inglesa

Patagonia is renowned for spectacular skies

snow-capped volcanoes, the perfectly coned Osorno and the ragged Hornopiren, pierce the otherwise flat horizon.

The further south you go, the wilder the scenery gets, with not even an occasional village to temper the knowledge that you are venturing into relatively unknown territory. Darwin and his fellow explorers found the islands to be impenetrable, saying: 'As for the woods, our faces, hands and shin-bones all bore witness to the maltreatment we received in merely attempting to penetrate their forbidden recesses.'

At times the channels between the islands narrow down alarmingly, to the point where it seems impossible for the ship to avoid running aground, but the greatest excitement of the journey is reserved for the grand, open and often savage spaces of the Southern Ocean. The crossing of the Golfo de Penas – literally the Gulf of Grief – takes on legendary proportions, and the hours leading up to it are filled with nervous talk about what lies ahead and the recounting of second- and third-hand tales about travellers' experiences in the

Expert crew are needed to negotiate the hazardous waterways

past. The passenger-liaison officer adds weight to the stories by handing out free seasickness tablets.

What you get is pot luck – being rolled around in your bunk all night with the occasional airborne experience on some larger waves is a good crossing, according to the truck drivers – but it is likely that those tablets will come in handy for many. The reward for surviving the gulf is a spellbinding landscape of wild mountains, icebergs and glaciers, and waters full of seals, humpback whales and dolphins. These waters were the ancient trading routes of the fearsome

Safety equipment is hopefully not needed   There is plenty of time to relax

Teheuleche Indians, the only native South American people to
successfully resist the Spanish invaders. The last of their descendants,
the Kawéskars, still live in scattered settlements along the southern
channels, and the ship stops at its namesake village, Puerto Edén, to
drop off goods and supplies, giving those on board a chance to buy
arts and crafts from the villagers.

The last night on board is disco night, and as Patagonia puts on its
unique extravaganza of spectacular dusk skies – well, you simply have
to be there to understand what effect four days on a ship, a severely

When the sun shines, everyone gets out on deck

Puerto Montt lies opposite Chiloé Island

depleted store of Gato Negro wine and some classic Abba tunes can have on normally grown-up and sensible people. It is a hilarious reminder that money doesn't always buy you the best experiences.

In the morning light, the captain skilfully guides the ship through the unbelievably slim Angostura Inglesa (English Narrows) and into majestic Last Hope Sound with its otherworldly cloud formations. The tin roofs of Puerto Natales, your journey's end, glisten on the nearby shore but nobody will be in a rush to disembark.

The ship is a commercial ferry too

ⓘ ···

The Navimag ship sails in each direction once a week – it is probably best to go from north to south as the scenery just gets wilder as you approach Puerto Natales. Tickets can be booked online directly from Navimag (see page 255) and prices vary depending on the type of cabin you want and the number of people sharing it. Prices include food, but it is a good idea to take your own snacks as well as drinks. You can fly to Puerto Montt from Santiago, or take a 16-hour bus ride in a very comfortable coach.

Snowy peaks line the fjords

Dawn is a perfect time to see mirror-like lakes

The enduring influence of the English poet William Wordsworth (1770–1850) pervades the craggy mountains and lush green valleys of the Lake District in north-west England, one of the country's premier hiking destinations. And a walk along the William Wordsworth Way provides a memorable opportunity to find out what so inspired the man who in 'Daffodils', perhaps his most famous poem, described how he '... wandered lonely as a cloud ...'.

Sunrise over the Lakeland fells

While many writers who found inspiration in the Lake District came to the region from other parts of the country, Wordsworth was born there, in 1770, in the market town of Cockermouth. After spending much of his childhood in Penrith, on the north-eastern edge of Lakeland, he went to school in Hawkshead. It was during his eight-year stay here that his interest in poetry was ignited, thanks to its natural beauty, set among the rolling fields and woods on the fringes of Esthwaite Water, and the encouragement of his headmaster. His early morning walks before school engendered his love for wanderings in the Lake District later in life.

Derwent Water

The William Wordsworth Way, a circular route contained within the Lake District National Park, starts and finishes in Cockermouth, and covers about 290 km in its full loop through Keswick, Penrith, Windermere, Hawkshead and Buttermere. It can take up to two weeks to walk it in its entirety, but it can be readily divided into significantly shorter sections, or even sliced into day hikes to fit your schedule or focus of interest.

The official starting point for the walk is outside Wordsworth House on Main Street in Cockermouth. It does not take long to leave the bustle of the busy market town behind as you head out on a five-hour section to Keswick. En route, you pass through Low Lorton village, where the yew tree that is the focus of Wordsworth's 'Yew Trees' once stood behind the village hall. Keswick is at the northern end of majestic, 5-km-long Derwent Water, a modern-day favourite with lovers of watersports and the third largest lake in the Lake District. It is graced by five islands and the views over the surrounding fern-clad slopes are breathtaking as you continue along the trail, beneath Cat Bells peak on its western shore. Avid hikers can detour to Applethwaite and ascend Skiddaw (931 metres).

By day three, you will be heading for what was probably the poet's favourite mountain: the magnificent Helvellyn (905 metres) between Thirlmere and Ullswater. If you have a head for heights, enjoy scrambling (and weather conditions allow) don't miss the spectacular and dramatic descent along Striding Edge, an arcing, knife-edge ridge that leads down from the summit. Wordsworth expounded on Helvellyn's majesty in 'Fidelity':

> Thither the rainbow comes – the cloud –
> And mists that spread the flying shroud;
> And sunbeams; and the sounding blast,
> That, if it could, would hurry past;
> But that enormous barrier holds it fast.

Wordsworth's gravesite at Grasmere church

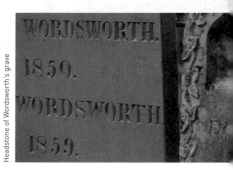
Headstone of Wordsworth's grave

Dove Cottage in Grasmere

Grasmere church

While the official route goes east to Penrith from Glenridding, it is possible to head south instead and rejoin the trail as it heads through beautiful hills towards Grasmere, Wordsworth's actual and spiritual home. After spending 12 years away from Lakeland, at Cambridge University, the poet returned there in 1799 and, with his sister Dorothy, bought Dove Cottage in Grasmere. It was here, inspired by the hills around White Moss Common and picturesque Rydal Water, that he penned several of his most famous poems, including 'Daffodils' and

The exposed Striding Edge ridge on Helvellyn

'Intimations of Immortality from Recollections of Early Childhood'. After 14 years at Dove Cottage Wordsworth moved his family to nearby Rydal Mount, but on his death in 1850 he was buried at Grasmere church. A visit to his grave, which lies alongside those of his wife Mary, his sister Dorothy and his daughter Dora is a must.

From Grasmere, the route heads west to ascend the lofty Langdale Pikes, a walk highly thought of by Wordsworth and which he described in 'The Excursion'. The hike up the Pikes is tough, but you

will be rewarded by superb views over the splendid Langdale Valley and Dungeon Ghyll. From Ambleside, another major tourist centre, the walking gets easier as you head south and skirt above the east shore of Lake Windermere, the most famous of all the lakes. In the town of Windermere, and in neighbouring Bowness, there is plenty to see and do – enough to warrant stopping for a few days and resting your feet.

From Bowness, the trail takes you towards the western lakes, via a short ferry ride, and on through the extensive Grizedale Forest to Hawkshead. You will find this part of the Lake District is much quieter, and in many ways wilder, than the places you have walked through so far. Wordsworth found much inspiration here, and today it remains a favourite with many locals. From Hawkshead to Boot, the route continues past Coniston Water, where a worthwhile detour from the official trail takes you up Coniston Old Man, an iconic Lakeland peak.

Farm fields from Cats Bells

North of Boot is Wasdale Head, a truly spectacular valley, near Wastwater, overlooked by England's highest peak: Scafell Pike (978 metres). As you return to Cockermouth you encounter some testing climbs towards the village of Buttermere. By now though, your legs will be well adapted to the rigours of Lakeland hiking and, hopefully, the scenery will have inspired you as much as it did Wordsworth himself.

ⓘ ···

The nearest international airport to the Lake District is Manchester. From there it is a one- or two-hour drive or train journey, depending on where you are heading. Although there are bus services between the main towns, hire a car if you want to move around quickly. The Lake District is notorious for its ever-changing weather, so it is essential to carry, at the very least, an extra layer of warm clothing and a waterproof jacket. There are excellent hiking maps, the most popular of which are the Ordnance Survey *Landranger* 1:50,000 series and *Explorer* 1:25,000 series. Both are readily available in main Lake District towns. In Howard Beck's guide, *The William Wordsworth Way* (Mainstream Publishing), the walk is organized so that each day ends in a place where accommodation of some kind is available.

Descending from Cats Bells

Cats Bells, near Derwent Water

Trans-Mongolian Railway
Moscow to Beijing

Take the epic, week-long Trans-Mongolian train ride from Russia's imposing capital, Moscow, across Mongolia's steppes and the Gobi Desert to Beijing and your daily commute to work will never seem quite the same again.

The Trans-Mongolian line stretches for almost 8000 km and is one of the three options available on what is commonly referred to as the Trans-Siberian Railway. The other two are the Trans-Manchurian train, which goes from Moscow to Beijing but skirts through Manchuria in China, instead of Mongolia; and the Trans-Siberian itself, which runs from Moscow to Vladivostok. The latter is primarily

Train guards at Ulan-Ude station, Russia

Gandantegchinlen Khiid Buddhist monastery, Ulaan Baatar

the reserve of die-hard railway fans, offering arguably fewer highlights and a longer journey than the Mongolian route. The Trans-Mongolian diverts south at Ulan Ude, near Lake Baikal's eastern shore, towards Ulaan Baatar.

All three are real rail journeys rather than luxury trips, so be prepared to mix with the locals and forgo home comforts. The train stops only to pick up or set down passengers, and to allow sellers of snacks and fur hats to fill the platform and your window. There are no sightseeing halts, so if you want to stay at any of the places en route you will have to leave the train and wait for the next one – which, unless you stop over at a major city, could arrive as much as a week

later. Careful planning is needed if you go independently, but there are tour companies who will organize the journey for you.

The idea for a great railway network running east from Moscow was driven by trade and the opening up of the port of Vladivostok in the late 19th century, and work on the railway began in 1891, under Tsar Alexander III. The route was fully open within 15 years, thanks largely to a huge workforce of soldiers and prison labourers. Moscow itself is an intriguing city, and it is well worth spending a couple of days exploring it before you board the train. If you only do one thing there, don't miss the spectacular St Basil's Cathedral in

Attendant on the train

St Basil's Cathedral, Red Square, Moscow

Lenin's tomb in Moscow

Red Square, with its bulbous towers and eye-smacking colour scheme.

As you board the Trans-Mongolian train at the city's pinnacle-roofed but otherwise dour Yaroslavski station, smartly uniformed staff will greet you with, if you watch carefully, a smile – on the whole, however, they are friendly and will help where and when they can. Depending on how you have decided to travel, you then settle into your comfortable first-class cabin with two beds or your second-class one with four beds – two above two. Every train has a restaurant car that changes depending on the country you are in. Most of the time the food is reasonable at best – airline standard – and never shows any signs of alerting the Michelin inspectors.

After leaving Moscow the train rattles and clanks its way eastwards through open country towards Yekaterinburg; established by Catherine the Great in 1721, this is now a large industrial city. Life on board is perhaps more interesting than the scenery during this first part of the journey, as you meet local Russians, Siberians – they understandably see themselves as a people apart, given that their region was for many years a place of exile – Chinese, and a whole raft of low-budget European and Antipodean travellers. The Russians and Siberians, in particular, have a hearty love of life and all its trappings, especially vodka. No night passes by without this social drink forming the basis of an impromptu gathering somewhere on the train.

Napoleonic cannon at the Kremlin

Pagoda at the Summer Palace, Beijing

A few days into the journey, after passing through sparsely populated lands punctuated by the occasional concrete city skyline and sprinkled with spruce forests, you reach the first major highlight. Just beyond the city of Irkutsk, an important trading centre, lie the vast waters of Baikal, the world's deepest lake and the largest in Asia. Just shy of 645 km long, and 80 km wide and 1637 metres deep, it is more like a sea than a lake and contains around one-fifth of the planet's freshwater supplies. With a distinct geological history that dates back around 250 million years, and a large number of endemic creatures, including the Baikal seal, calling it home, it has deservedly been accorded World Heritage status by UNESCO. If you are going to stop over at any point, Lake Baikal is well worth considering.

Mao still overlooks Tiananmen Square in Beijing

Trekking on the Great Wall of China

Even if you don't have time to stop, there are great views as the train continues east along the lake shore towards Ulan Ude where the Trans-Mongolian departs from the other Trans-Siberian Railway routes. Over 5500 km into the journey, the city has a strong Buddhist tradition and a fascinating museum of history where many religious artefacts, including a beautiful Tibetan atlas of medicine, were stored when they were banned during the Soviet era. Over the next 12 hours or so, as you pass through the section from Ulan Ude to the Russian–Mongolian border at Naushki, you enter barren and rolling steppe lands that add a real feeling of wilderness to the train ride.

If you have travelled anywhere in the world in the last five years or so, you may have noticed that it is now much easier to cross borders. In an attempt to encourage tourism, most countries have reduced bureaucracy and the need for visas. On this trip, you will be reminded of how it used to be. It seems to take an age to fill out forms, get eyed up and down by customs officers, and then queue and queue again to get your stamps.

Once in Mongolia, the landscape remains the same but you will start to see groups of *gers*, the traditional round tents used by herder

Monkey king at the Beijing Opera

Seventeen Arch Bridge to the Summer Palace, Beijing

The chaotic streets of Beijing

families, dotting the gentle green hills and valleys. By the time you reach Ulaan Baatar you will probably be eager for a break from the train, and many travellers opt to spend a few days or more there. The city itself is relatively uninspiring but there are tours to the surrounding steppe lands where you can meet Mongolian families, and get a real taste of Mongolian life – salty yaks' butter and fermented mares' milk included.

Back on the train, the forbidding Gobi Desert awaits to the south of Ulaan Baatar. It is a good idea to keep your eyes peeled because it won't be long before you see camels and more *ger* settlements. By the end of the sixth day on board the train you reach the Mongolian–Chinese border at Erlyan. Be prepared for more paperwork and queuing, and the bizarre scene where the carriages are lifted so that their wheel bogies can be changed – the railway gauge in China is different to those in Russia and Mongolia.

The 800-km journey south passes close enough to the Great Wall to give you a glimpse of it, before the train rolls into Beijing. The Trans-Mongolian train ride is an unusual journey, and certainly an unforgettable one that will probably furnish you with stories that will amaze your friends for a long time to come.

ⓘ ....

While it is possible to buy train tickets in Moscow, or Beijing if you are doing the journey in reverse, it is advisable to book before you leave home, especially if you want to travel first class. Make sure you seek advice on visas well in advance – you may be able to get just a transit visa for Mongolia. You will almost certainly need a visa to enter China and they are not issued on the border. Many tour companies in Europe and North America offer itineraries based on the train journey, including overnight stops at major cities en route. If you want a relatively hassle-free trip it is advisable to use one of them. It is worth taking extra snacks on board in case the food doesn't agree with you or leaves you feeling hungry.

Impressive pagoda turrets guard the corners of Beijing's Forbidden City

In one of Mother Nature's most impressive extravaganzas, the arrival of fall in New England sends an extraordinary swathe of amber, yellow and red sweeping across the tree tops. Although autumn colours can be seen around the world, here a unique combination of climate, tree species and terrain makes the display possibly the most spectacular on the planet – and a week or so driving around the region an unforgettable experience.

Driving into the White Mountains

Because it is an all-natural show, it is impossible to predict accurately from year to year where the best colours will be and, more importantly, when they will appear, so it helps to have a flexible holiday plan. October is usually the prime month in New England – a region that borders Canada and includes the states of New Hampshire, Vermont and Maine – and the blanket of colour spreads from north to south. There is no need to travel blind, though, as there are several websites that track the colours as they peak.

Reflections in Lake Winnipesaukee

Driving through fall colours
New England, USA

Sunset on Lake Champlain

Changes in colour are often localized and it can come down to particular roads being better than others if you want to catch them at their best. Displays can also alter fairly dramatically from day to day, and from one valley or mountain top to the next. Altitude plays a big part in how the colours spread, with trees at high levels tending to turn before ones in valleys. So, get yourself a good map, stock up on the latest information and tracking the changes will turn out to be part of the fun, like a relaxing form of tornado chasing. The lure of the leaf – enthusiasts are deemed 'leaf peepers' by locals – will take you to parts of New England no ordinary tour will reach.

A classic circuit from the city of Boston takes you north-west into Vermont, back east to catch the display in the dramatic White Mountains of northern New Hampshire and then south again to the beautiful lakes region near Laconia. It takes in most of the best areas and is loosely threaded by the mighty Connecticut River. Although the interstate highways are tempting for their directness and speed, the old roads, which often run parallel, offer the most absorbing drives.

Highway 12 takes you north along the river, past a series of New England's trademark covered wooden bridges, to Lebanon. From here, there is a stunning drive on Highway 4 through mountains and Woodstock to Rutland. Sweeping views southwards to the golden hills of the Green Mountain National Forest make stopping a necessity – your only problem will be to choose between several spectacularly located restaurants.

From Rutland, you wind across rolling hills to impressive Lake Champlain on the New York State border. With its shoreline dotted with idyllic retreats, it is a lovely place to watch the gentle warm rays of sunset wash across the water. Heading back eastwards, Highway 302 takes you across the Connecticut River and into the most beautiful part of New Hampshire: the White Mountain National

Hiking in the woods near Holderness

Rapids in the White Mountains

Holderness School

Forest. With 1916-metre Mount Washington topping the rugged peaks that pierce the skyline, the park is one of the prime places to see the autumn colours. A good way to access the area is along the twisting Highway 112, or Kancamagus Highway, from Woodsville to yet another Woodstock – rather confusingly, several village and town names are repeated throughout New England.

Long, warm summers lead to brighter red leaves

If you are there at the right time the vista is breathtaking, with towering mountains swathed in a forest of red, gold, bronze, yellow and green. Most of the leaves change colour because of the reduction in chlorophyll created by the cooler temperatures of the approaching winter. The brilliant reds of the maples, however, have their origins in the warmth of summer when the sunlight produces sugar in the leaves. The warmer the summer, the bigger the explosion of autumn reds.

One not-to-be-missed sight in the White Mountains is the Flume Gorge just off Highway 3, north of Lincoln. A short hiking trail leads through forest and past a tumultuous waterfall to a stunning, red, covered bridge, built in 1886, over the Pemigewasset River, and continues into the dramatic narrow gorge. There are numerous other trails, and walking any one of them provides a perspective to experiencing the colours that is different from a car. Back behind the wheel, other roads in the park lead over rocky mountain passes at Franconia Notch and Crawford Notch, both of which are worth exploring.

Trees alongside Route 109

Maple tree in White Mountains

Maple leaf on Squam Lake

189

Forest over Squam Lake, Holderness

In contrast, the land to the south of the White Mountains is more gentle and is dominated by a sprawl of lakes, including vast Lake Winnipesaukee. The small village of Holderness on the edge of Squam Lake, where the quaint general store sells a mouth-watering selection of home-made fudge, is a good place to begin a half-day circumnavigation of the lakes. A short drive along Highway 25 takes you to the tranquil fishing village of Center Harbor and on to Route 109, which follows a mazy path down the east shore of Winnipesaukee lake. Here the trees are mainly golden and bronze, bathing the road in a warm glow when the sun shines through them. From Alton Bay you can make your way up the western shore and

Heavy autumn rain swells the rivers

Covered bridge over the Pemigewasset River

back to Holderness, where watching the moon rise over the lake from your motel balcony is the perfect end to your journey through Mother Nature's autumn colour festival.

ⓘ ....

Although many companies offer guided tours of the New England fall colours, it is easy enough to rent a car in Boston and devise your own tour. The relevant state tourist offices can offer extensive advice on choosing routes. Accommodation in the region's smaller towns and villages can be fully booked during the peak weeks of October, but may be available in major towns on the interstate highways. One of the best websites for tracking the colour changes is www.foliagenetwork.com, where volunteers report regularly on conditions across the region. They also suggest drives that will catch the best colours.

On the Road to Mandalay

Ayeyarwady River, Myanmar

Ananda Pagoda in Bagan

With thousands of dramatic pagodas, a strong Buddhist culture and ancient rural landscapes, Myanmar is a unique travel gem. There is no better way to see what inspired Rudyard Kipling's poem 'Mandalay' than a luxurious voyage along the Ayeyarwady River from Bagan to Mandalay.

Once part of the British Empire, when the country was known as Burma, Myanmar gained its independence in 1948 and, after 1962, became relatively isolated under the socialist military regime of Ne Win. Frozen in time by decades of limited access for outsiders, in recent years it has started to open itself to visitors. Its cultural treasures and peaceful charm are, as Kipling noticed on his first visit, '... quite unlike any other land you know about'. And perhaps the most

Sunset over pagodas in Bagan

spectacular of Myanmar's treasures is the extensive, golden-topped
Swedagon Pagoda in the capital Yangon (the city formerly called
Rangoon) – a must-see before you head further north to travel
the river.

If the Swedagon Pagoda is breathtaking in its size, the sight of the
more than three thousand pagodas that await you in the beautiful old
capital city of Bagan (Pagan), a 1½-hour flight north, is awe-inspiring.
The starting point for your four-day voyage up the Ayeyarwady
(Irrawaddy) to Mandalay, Bagan lies on the river's vast plain and its
sensuous, pointed-topped pagodas spike the skyline from wherever
you view them. The city became the capital of a powerful Burmese
dynasty in the 11th century and flourished over the next 200 years;

Dawn balloon ride, Bagan

Hot-air balloon rides are a great way to see Bagan's temples

at its peak it boasted over 40,000 pagodas. Most of them are now completely ruined, but visitors are still spoilt for choice – you will feel like a Victorian explorer as you come across rarely visited 800-year-old, red-brick pagodas, crumbling and half-overgrown. More obvious highlights are the golden Buddha statues of the Ananda Pagoda and the fragile, ancient mural of the Buddha's life that fills the walls of the Gubyaukgyi Temple.

Bagan is also famous for its arts and crafts and is the production centre for the country's impressive lacquerware. You could spend all day shopping in Nyaung-Oo market but the real beauty of the city comes with sunset. The sun's rays wash the pagodas in a golden light and if you climb to the top of one of them you'll get a grandstand view. With ox carts working the patchwork of fields, people cycling and mauve-robed monks walking back to their monasteries, it is a scene of pure serenity; it is barely believable that such a way of life still exists in our modern world.

Dusk over Bagan and the Ayeyarwady River

You will probably be thankful, though, that the best aspects of this modern world can be found on board the exquisite *Road to Mandalay*. The ship offers luxury accommodation and fine dining, and as you sail up the Ayeyarwady you can relax on deck and watch age-old scenes of everyday living unfold on its banks. The river is the backbone of Myanmar and, as the roads are poor at best, it is still the main way of getting people and goods around the country. Timber

Novice monks at Shwe Kyet Yet

Carving bamboo at Bagan lacquerware shop

Zayar Theingi Nunnery, Mandalay

Fish stall at Nyaung-Oo market, Bagan

Door carving at Shwenandaw Monastery, Mandalay

Nuns collecting alms in Bagan

Lacquerware store, Bagan

Marble buddhas, Bagan

Rowing on Taungthaman Lake

barges mix it with fishermen in dugout canoes, even though the Ayeyarwady is so wide that there is plenty of space for everyone. The pace of travel is sublime and at dusk, as the stars become bright pinpoints in the inky sky, the ship seems to glide through the water with effortless ease.

By day three you pull into the small village of Shwe Kyet Yet, the main mooring port for the *Road to Mandalay* and just a 15-minute drive from Mandalay itself. Deliberately chosen to avoid the hustle of this large city, the mainly bamboo village is a lovely place for wandering. In the early morning the monks from its monastery queue up to collect alms from the villagers, while schoolgirls play skipping games, old men mend bicycles and old women cook food in clay ovens.

In Mandalay ancient wooden monasteries, like the ornately carved Shwenandaw Monastery, stand close to huge temple complexes, the most revered of which is the one in honour of Mahamuni. Inside, worshippers constantly cover his statue with fresh gold leaf. This is

Monk on U Bein bridge, Taungthaman Lake

Monks collecting alms in Shwe Kyet Yet

Nun praying, Yangon

made locally and it is an eye-opening experience to visit one of the factories and see just how much bashing it takes to make gold so thin. At sunset make your way to the long wooden U Bein bridge over Taungthaman Lake. Monks, nuns, fishermen and cyclists make their way across its stilted wooden beams, forming perfect silhouettes against the dusk sky.

Further upriver, reached by a smaller ferry boat, is the impressive Mingun Pagoda, an unfinished project built in about 1790 to house one of the Buddha's teeth. Its massive base is bigger than those of the other pagodas in the region and it would have been three times higher than any of them. The views from the top are worth the testing climb up steep steps. Mingun is also home to the world's largest working bell – the biggest is in Russia but it no longer functions.

There can be no more fitting place to bid farewell to Myanmar than from atop the Sagaing Hills, overlooking Mandalay and Shwe Kyet Yet where the *Road to Mandalay* is moored. With temples on either side and stretching out to the horizon, and the glinting lights of the ship piercing the twilight sky, it is easy to see what inspired Rudyard Kipling's famous poem about this beautiful, unspoilt place, and its refrain 'Come you back to Mandalay ...'

The *Road to Mandalay* takes four days to sail from Bagan to Mandalay and three days to travel the opposite way, downriver. A longer 12-day tour to Bhamo in the north of the country is available in August. The ship is owned by the Orient Express group so food, service and accommodation are of the highest standard. You can fly to Yangon from Bangkok or Singapore and there are good flights from Yangon to Bagan and Mandalay. Mandalay airport is new, while Yangon was having a new international terminal built at the time of writing. Excellent accommodation in Yangon can be found at The Governor's Residence, which is now a hotel. US dollars are the best currency and credit cards are not widely accepted, even in Yangon.

The *Road to Mandalay*

Buddhas in Sagaing Hills

Driving the Uyuni Salt Flat
Altiplano, Bolivia

Few places on the planet are as wild and difficult to access as the awe-inspiring salt flat around Uyuni in the south-western deserts of Bolivia's Altiplano. With few surfaced roads, exploring the world's largest expanse of salt requires a four-wheel-drive vehicle and a sense of adventure. The rewards are startling, as you see volcanoes in the majestic Sajama National Park, encounter unspoilt Aymara Indian villages and experience the unique thrill of driving across endless salt with virtually nothing to be seen on the entire horizon.

The starting point for any journey in Bolivia is La Paz, which, stunningly located at 3600 metres, is the world's highest capital. It won't take you long to be aware of the altitude – you begin breathing heavily on arrival at the airport – and it is worth planning a day or two

Sajama volcano, Bolivia's highest peak at 6549 metres

Driving into Sajama National Park

Llamas in Sajama National Park

in the city to acclimatize before heading elsewhere. Built in a huge bowl surrounded by 6000-metre-high, snow-capped Andean peaks, La Paz is a constant buzz of activity, with plenty of markets, cultural sights and fiestas to keep you entertained. It is claimed that there are three fiestas for every day of the year.

There are several routes for getting to the Salar de Uyuni (Uyuni Salt Flat) but a good option is to go via the less-frequented gem: the Sajama National Park, south-west of La Paz and right on the Chilean border. Even with an asphalt road going all the way to the park entrance the drive takes four or five hours. With only occasional small villages along the way, often overlooked by ancient, mud-brick Indian

Indian women herding donkeys to Sajama village

tombs, it gives you a sense of Bolivia's vastness and the awesome-
ness of its wilderness. It is a country ripe for exploring.

The national park is named after Bolivia's highest peak, the 6549-
metre Sajama volcano, which, thanks to its isolation, dominates the
landscape for miles around. A thick, glacial cap drapes across its
summit and its blackened slopes plunge steeply to the Altiplano
desert. Those with a head for heights and a guide can spend a couple
of days hiking and climbing to its top. For the hardy Aymara and
Quechua Indians, Sajama is a sacred mountain representing the head
of Muruata, who was beheaded by the god Wiracocha as a punish-
ment for being too arrogant.

Sajama village itself, tucked below the volcano, is a hotchpotch of mud-brick houses, many of which are painted in bright greens, whites and yellows, possibly to add life to the dusty desert landscape. From the village you can drive across the river to a nearby geothermal valley where hot geysers bubble and mud pools boil. With steam rising from the pools and various streams, the scene resembles a battlefield; but the only thing likely to attack you here is the sulphur fumes. If you are lucky, a full moon will rise behind Sajama at dusk, bathing the landscape in an ethereal silver glow.

Reaching the next village, Sabaya, calls for an early start and a drive along a little-used track that skirts the Chilean border, via Macoya and Tunupa. The ride is rough at times but spotting wildlife will be a distraction. Small groups of nervous and flighty vicuna

Driving on to Salar de Coipasa

Vast expanse of Salar de Uyuni

wander the plain. By the 1970s these small members of the camel family had been hunted almost to extinction for their valuable fur. The population has recovered now, thanks to major conservation efforts across the Andes.

From Sabaya, a one-street village way off the beaten tourist track, it is a few kilometres to the Salar de Coipasa, the second-largest salt flat after Uyuni, which boasts a host of small islands near the shore. Leaving the green and brown behind, and driving out along a causeway on to white salt for the first time is quite unnerving. Ahead there is nothing except distant mountains – this is definitely not a place for agoraphobics. The vehicle's wheels crack and crunch across the widespread hexagonal patterns, formed by the salt, that at times make the surface seem like crazy paving. The surface of Coipasa is less stable than that of Uyuni and so the temptation to drive off the main tracks should be resisted. Speeding across the flat is great fun and the route eventually takes you off the salt to Llica, close to the north-western edge of the Uyuni salt flat. Fuelled partly

Cacti grow on rocks above Salar de Uyuni

Sunset trek overlooking Salar de Uyuni

by illicit trade across the Chilean frontier, Llica is a 'happening' town in Altiplano terms, with a rapidly growing population. It is also among the best options outside Uyuni for finding a bed for the night.

The following morning, after checking out at the slightly bizarre military checkpoint at the entrance to the salt flat, it is time to head out into the big white yonder. Salar de Uyuni was part of a giant, prehistoric lake – Minchin – which dried up and deposited a thick layer of salt, covering about 12,000 sq. km and measuring over 130 km across. Near the centre it is possible to find places with an almost perfect 360-degree view of flatness, where you can hear the true meaning of a deafening silence. Occasionally you happen upon a cactus-covered island, shimmering like the mirage of a spaceship. Hike to the top of any of them for a literally breathtaking view.

Sunset over Lake Poopó, near Oruro

ⓘ ⸺⸺⸺⸺⸺⸺⸺⸺⸺⸺⸺⸺⸺⸺⸺⸺⸺⸺⸺

Several companies based in Uyuni town run standard three-to-four-day tours to the salt flat, but they can seem a little rushed. Using one of the specialist La Paz-based adventure companies, such as Andean Summits, allows you to tailor-make a tour with the freedom to explore further and visit places like the Sajama National Park en route. Allow at least a week to explore the region more fully. There are also one-way salt flat tours that go through to Chile. To reach Uyuni, either take a bus from La Paz or any other major town in the southern region, or go to Oruro by bus and take the slow but characterful train from there to Uyuni. Be aware that travelling around the Uyuni region is generally slow because of the total lack of surfaced roads. Accommodation is also very basic.

The Eastern & Oriental Express
Singapore to Bangkok

Winding its way northwards through the tropical rainforests, rice paddies and limestone escarpments of Singapore, Malaysia and Thailand, the *Eastern & Oriental Express* whisks you back to a time when exotic train journeys were a romantic luxury.

Starting in Singapore, it follows a historic 2030-km route that, over three days, takes you through the western lowlands of Malaysia to the country's capital Kuala Lumpur, and onwards across the Thailand border. Near Bangkok, it makes a detour to cross the famous bridge on the River Kwai, scene of one of the most compelling stories from the Second World War.

Singapore is a majestic modern city of skyscrapers, a major seaport and, with its Chinese, Malay and Indian influences, a

Dinner aboard the train at Kuala Lumpur station

melting pot of Asian cultures. It is well worth spending a day or two here before setting out on your journey. Once you arrive at Keppel Road station, in itself a downbeat affair which, strangely, still belongs to Malaysia, the *Eastern & Oriental Express* experience begins. Porters take your luggage, check-in staff escort you to your elegant carriage and ever-smiling cabin attendants ease you into life on board with a cocktail. Inside the compartments, rosewood furniture and ornate lamps make for a warm welcome, and many guests find the lure of watching the world go by in air-conditioned comfort too hard to resist.

However, it would be a folly to miss out on the luscious viewing provided by the open-air observation car at the rear of the train. The concrete towers of Singapore are soon left behind as you cross the

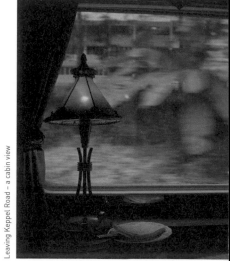

Leaving Keppel Road – a cabin view

Strait of Johor and are replaced by the deep green, large-leaf plants of the rainforest. The railway line is almost entirely single track, and at times the vegetation presses in close enough to clip both sides of the carriages as the train threads its way towards Kuala Lumpur. A short stop in Malaysia's capital in the balmy early evening allows you to hop

Threading through the lush Thai landscape

off for a quick view of the 88-storey Petronas Twin Towers, which, at 452 metres high, are the world's tallest linked towers.

Back on board it is time for the first of many exquisite meals – so good that they justify leaving any thoughts about diets for a later date. They are often based on regional specialities, so you get to taste Asia as well as see it roll past the window. In the sumptuous dining cars, where smart dress is essential, the elegant heyday of rail travel comes to life. Of course, no luxury train is complete without a resident pianist in the bar car, and as the *Eastern & Oriental Express* clacks and rumbles its way up the Malay Peninsula you can dance the night away to an eclectic mix of jazz and modern classics.

The train keeps up a surprising speed and by the morning of the second day you wake around sunrise to find yourself surrounded by water as the railway line crosses a very narrow causeway over a lake. With daylight, the seemingly endless rice paddies glint into life as a small army of workers stoops into the water to plant or pick rice while others drive cattle-drawn, wooden ploughs monotonously back and forth in arrow-straight lines. Whenever the train comes to a level crossing the drivers of scores of mopeds – a favourite mode of transport – queue up at the barriers, flashing smiles at you whenever they catch your eye. It is an endearing snapshot of normal daily life.

As it nears the top of Malaysia the train diverts westwards to Butterworth on the coast of the Andaman Sea for a short excursion to the island of Penang and its colonial capital, George Town. Once a British settlement owned by the East India Company, George Town is now a bustling market town and is reached via a 15-minute ferry ride. Without doubt the best way to get around it is by trishaw, enthusiastically pedalled by a driver who will take pleasure in pointing out any building of significance.

Back aboard the express, the Thailand border beckons as you pass through a marvellous landscape of towering, limestone

Cyclist on the line in Thailand

Rice paddies line much of the route

rock-islands. As the sun drops rapidly to the horizon, the observation car allows a view of golden rays glinting down the side of the train as it runs between densely vegetated, green cuttings. The Thai border comes and goes with only a brief stop for customs formalities, and while you sleep in your gently rocking compartment the *Eastern & Oriental Express* continues its speedy route north towards Kanchanaburi, junction for the line to the bridge on the River Kwai.

Built in 1942 by the Japanese, using prisoners of war, the multi-span bridge formed a key part of the notorious Burma–Thailand railway. Tens of thousands of prisoners and locals died building the line, succumbing to heat, starvation or disease. The Allied forces bombed the bridge repeatedly but finally destroyed it only in 1944. It is at the centre of Pierre Boulle's novel, *The Bridge on the River Kwai*, and was made famous by David Lean's film of the same name. An excellent museum, the Thailand–Burma Railway Centre, at nearby Ban Lin Chang, tells the true and harrowing story of how the line was built. It is not to be missed.

Not long after leaving the River Kwai the train rumbles into the outskirts of Bangkok, where shanty houses are built to within inches of the railway line. A night out in the city centre, with its bright lights and 24-hour lifestyle, is a vibrant way to end this exquisite rail journey across the heart of south-east Asia.

ⓘ ··

The *Eastern & Oriental Express* is operated by the Orient Express company and runs between Singapore and Bangkok, and also on to Chiang Mai in the north of Thailand. The journey to Bangkok lasts about 58 hours – you spend two nights on board – but this can vary depending on other rail traffic, and track or weather conditions. The train also operates in the opposite direction, from Bangkok to Singapore. Standard national train services travel the same route but do not offer any comforts. Singapore is served by about 20 major airlines.

The *Eastern & Oriental Express* crossing the bridge on the River Kwai

Copán, in Honduras, is known as the 'Paris' of the Mayan world

Snaking its way through the rainbow-coloured culture and mysterious history of the Mayan civilization in Central America, La Ruta Maya takes you to enchanting ruined cities where ancient pyramids tower above the jungle canopy, to one of the world's most beautiful lakes and into villages and towns that are still home to Mayan communities.

Dawn over the ballcourt at Copán, Honduras

Although the intriguing story of the Maya dates back well over 1500 years, La Ruta Maya is a recent initiative aimed at easing the way for travellers to trace the civilization through four countries that share the old Mayan world: Mexico, Guatemala, Belize and Honduras. The route is loosely defined, so there aren't any definitive maps. You can travel along it by road (and in parts by river) for just a few days, or several weeks. Some places, though, are not to be missed, including the ruined cities of Palenque, Tikal and Copán, the beautiful colonial town of San Cristobal de las Casas and the thriving Mayan villages sprinkled around the shores of majestic Lake Atitlan.

Girls parading at Santiago Atitlan, Guatemala

The Mayan civilization rose to prominence around 400 AD, reached its zenith a few hundred years later, and then suffered a cataclysmic decline towards the end of the millennium. The exact causes of its demise are still unclear. At its height it was one of the most sophisticated civilizations on the planet, utilizing accurate cosmological observations and inventing a complex calendar, the Calendar Round, which included the notion of a 365-day year. The Maya built great cities dominated by imposing temples, and traded over immense distances with other peoples, possibly even with the Chinese. Theirs was no idyllic existence in a rainforest paradise, though. They practised human sacrifice to appease their gods, and rival cities fought bloody battles that became more aggressive as the civilization developed.

The busy Mayan market at Solola, near Lake Atitlan

Figures of Commandant Marcos, leader of Chiapas' Zapatista rebels

As there is no strictly defined Ruta Maya you can start your journey anywhere, and Palenque, in southern Mexico, is as good a place as any. Tucked into the foothills of the Chiapas mountains, on the edge of a misty rainforest, it was one of the most beautiful of the Mayan cities. With the signature, white elegant tower of its palace, and the sculpted roof-comb decorations that top off the surrounding temples, it exhibits some of the civilization's finest architecture. Clamber inside the Temple of the Inscriptions to see the tomb of Lord Pacal, Palenque's most glorious leader. The exquisitely carved lid of the sarcophagus features him on his final journey from life to death along the sacred Ceiba tree.

No visit to the region is complete without heading up through the mountains to the colonial town of San Cristobal de las Casas. Still the centre of a thriving Mayan community, its markets are awash with colourful crafts and the women are dressed in their vibrant traditional clothing. It is also possible to visit some of the surrounding villages for an even deeper taste of Mayan life. In particular, tiny

Chamula features a wonky old white church with a rainbow doorway, which is now used by Mayan shamans.

Some of the most powerful cities were in what is now northern Guatemala, most easily accessed from Mexico via the Yucatan Peninsula and Belize, and among them is the jewel in the Ruta Maya crown: Tikal. Set in a dense rainforest where howler monkeys roar and toucans swoop from tree to tree, Tikal was the New York of the Mayan world. Ruled by characters such as Great Jaguar Paw and Curl Snout, it was a major power base. Exploring there is quite magical, and it is worth staying overnight to watch the sun set over the rainforest from one of its six central pyramids. The largest of these mighty structures, Temple IV, soars about 70 metres into the sky, and climbing the steep, oversized steps to its summit is a challenge in itself.

Market at Chichicastenango, Guatemala

Early paper in San Cristobal de las Casas, Mexico

Mayan spirit masks in Panajachel, Lake Atitlan

A long bus ride or short flight south leads to the Guatemalan highlands and on to Lake Atitlan. Surrounded by volcanoes and traditional Mayan villages, it was described by author Aldous Huxley as the 'most beautiful lake in the world'. Few would argue. A peaceful boat trip takes you to the villages, each of which has its unique traditional dress, a kaleidoscope of reds, blues, purples and yellows.

A fitting finale to a journey along La Ruta Maya is the ruined city of Copán in northern Honduras. If Tikal was the New York of the Mayan world, Copán was its Paris. Set on a river bend in a broad valley, it boasts wonderfully proportioned temples and some of the

Embroidered shawl

Praying at Chichicastenango, Guatemala

finest Mayan standing-stone sculptures, or stelae. The Mayan civilization may have collapsed mysteriously, but the modern-day Maya and their ancient ruined cities are as compelling as ever.

(i) ···

Numerous tour operators offer trips based around La Ruta Maya, including tours that focus especially on the archaeology. Although it is possible to organize your own travel on public transport, this can be time-consuming and the journeys are long. Generally, there are very good accommodation options near most of the main sites. You could take in all four major centres of Palenque, Tikal, Lake Atitlan and Copán in a trip of 7–10 days.

Mayan ritual church in Chamula, Mexico

Camino de Santiago

Santiago de Compostela, Spain

Burgos Cathedral is a gothic gem

Pilgrims in Burgos

Lace up your walking boots for an epic, life-changing pilgrimage in the footsteps of St James that will take you, through beguiling landscapes and the historic cities and enchanting villages of northern Spain, to Santiago de Compostela.

The most popular route, the Camino Francés, starts in France at Saint-Jean-Pied-de-Port in the Pyrenees, is about 800 km long and takes about five weeks to walk. However, many people choose shorter sections, such as the one from León to Santiago, which can be completed in about 10 days. The good news if you don't have enough time for the entire journey is that walking anything over 100 km qualifies as a recognized pilgrimage, entitling you to a certificate on arrival in Santiago. No matter how far you choose to

Mountain views from O Cebreiro

Monument to the Pilgrim, O Cebreiro

hike, you will experience the camaraderie that bonds all pilgrims, whether it comes from sharing personal tales over a simple, hostel dinner or discussing the most effective remedies for blisters out on the trail.

An appealing reason, though daunting too, for setting off from Saint-Jean-Pied-de-Port is the breathtaking climb up over the Pyrenees via Rolando's Pass. It is a harsh start, even for the physically prepared. The scenery is spectacular, with verdant pastures dotted with traditional dark-red-and-white Basque houses, merging into the stark, ragged skyline of the high Pyrenean peaks. Once at the summit of the pass, marked with a simple stone monument and a pile of old wooden crosses, it is a relief to see the trail heading downwards through forests to the convent at Roncesvalles, in Spain.

In the lowlands the route passes through Pamplona, famed for its annual festival when bulls run through its streets, and on into

The first climbs over the Pyrenees are tough

La Rioja, one of Spain's premier wine-growing regions. A glass of wine at night is a popular pilgrim remedy for massaging aches away. When you enter the regional capital, Logroño, the cobbled street takes you to the pilgrim hostels, and then to the pilgrims' gate. West of the town modern roads have admittedly impinged on the beauty and serenity of parts of the route, but after passing the 13th-century church of San Juan de Ortega you reach the lovely city of Burgos, and beyond lies a more tranquil pilgrimage.

Burgos is rightly famed for its impressive Gothic cathedral and riverside parks, and it is well worth taking a day's break to explore it. The trail then follows old country lanes and footpaths across rolling hills and it is here, perhaps more than anywhere, that a grand sense of freedom washes over you. Enjoy it fully because ahead lies the mental challenge of crossing the plains of the León region. The walking is easy, but the monotony of the grand vista needs to be countered with a strong mind or good company.

Some people follow in St James' footsteps to get over major life traumas, some are looking for a new way to be and for others it is the one time in their busy lives when they can return to a simple way of living – eating, sleeping and walking. Whatever your reasons for making the pilgrimage, the distant goal of Santiago rarely leaves your mind for long, but somehow it becomes less important with each step you take.

Many places are worth stopping in en route, but few are as worthy as the city of León, capital of the kingdom of León in the 10th century. Architecture aficionados will also want to pause in Astorga, to its west, to see Gaudí's episcopal palace. In late spring the looming mountains of the Cordillera Cantábrica are carpeted with purple heather, and the route from Astorga passes through enchanting old-world villages like El Ganso and Rabanal del Camino.

Most pilgrims start the walk at Saint-Jean-Pied-de-Port in France

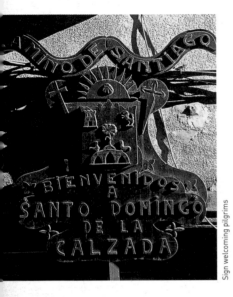

Sign welcoming pilgrims

The last big physical challenge is the daunting climb to O Cebreiro, a village that consists of a clutch of unique stone hostels, bars and shops with remarkable conical thatched roofs. The pilgrimage gains irresistible momentum from here on, and a monument of St James braced steadfastly against a roaring wind encourages pilgrims as they continue over the pass and into Galicia, in Spain's remote north-west corner.

Galicia is one of Spain's lesser-known regions. Lush, sparsely inhabited and laced with rivers and lakes, it is a fitting home-straight for this personal walk of a lifetime. Santiago de Compostela and its impressive cathedral beckon, and even the regular Galician rainstorms won't dampen your enthusiasm. Climbing the steps to the cathedral is a moving experience. As the bells toll, the daily Mass for

Ermita de la Virgen at Villafranca Montes de Oca

Portico of Glory at the cathedral in Santiago de Compostela

pilgrims begins and the golden statue of St James looks out over slightly bedraggled walkers and bikers surrounded by weathered backpacks. No matter how hard the struggle to get to their destination, there is not one pilgrim whose life remains unchanged by their journey.

ⓘ ··

Many maps and books detail the Camino de Santiago, one of the best of which is *The Road to Santiago Pilgrims Guide*, available from the Spanish Tourism Board. People of all ages and fitness levels take on the challenge of the pilgrimage, but it helps if you do at least a little training beforehand. There are other official pilgrim trails to Santiago de Compostela – the Camino del Norte, which runs across the northern coast of Spain, is one of the most popular.

Cathedral across Plaza do Obradoiro, Santiago de Compostela

Into the Sahara

Drâa Valley, Morocco

The drive crosses the High Atlas mountains

Inducing romantic images of nomads and camel caravans among endless, golden sand dunes, the Sahara is far more accessible today than it once was, yet it remains as alluring as ever. One of the best and easiest ways to get to it is to take a stirring four- or five-day drive across the High Atlas mountains and down the kasbah- and oasis-lined Drâa Valley in Morocco.

If the ever-creeping sands of the Sahara could have their way survival here would be all but impossible, yet in this harsh, dry region of North Africa even the tiniest amounts of water bring vivid life. The Oued

Morocco's highest road pass, Col du Tichka

Oued Drâa brings life to the valley, near Zagora

Drâa (Drâa River) emerges from the snow-topped High Atlas and, in fits and starts, carries its magical properties eastwards to the desert through the often abundant greenery of the palmeries on its banks. It once flowed all the way to the Atlantic Ocean but nowadays it is devoured by the Saharan sands near the tiny village of M'Hamid, the access point to the towering dunes of Erg Chagaga.

Set among the date palms, ancient fortified *ksour* and kasbahs house the once nomadic Berbers and Hassani, whose tribal traditions continue to form the backbone of community life. *Ksour* were

designed to defend entire communities whereas kasbahs tended to be for individual families – both are built from *pise* (dried mud). Over the centuries many have become dilapidated, but their softly eroded, crumbling walls only add to their charm.

The southern Moroccan city of Marrakech, famed for its souk and its bustling main square – Jemaa El Fna – filled with bizarre entertainers, is an ideal place to begin your journey. The Atlas mountains edge the city and the road towards them and the Drâa Valley town of Ouarzazate, 196 km and four hours away, soon begins its contorted ascent into the red earth and forests of the foothills. It is an exhilarating drive on a good surfaced road but steep drops, occasionally wayward traffic and often wayward humans and animals demand high levels of concentration. Panoramic views of the snow-laced mountains –

High Atlas road to Ouarzazate from Marrakech

The kasbah at Ait Benhaddou is a popular location for filmmakers

The oasis of Ait Benhaddou lies beneath the snow-capped High Atlas mountains

the loftiest in North Africa – are also a distraction as the road climbs to Tizi n'Tichka, at 2260 metres the highest pass in the Atlas.

If you have time there are several detours that are worth taking, the first of which is to Telouet just after the pass. The 20-km drive on a narrow, surfaced road – with bumpy bits en route – is a ride through a slice of geological history and in itself a good reason for making the side trip. As you plunge down into a valley the surrounding hills are a vast array of colours, from pink and red to green and black. In Telouet itself is a ruined, mansion-like kasbah that was built by the infamous Glaoui family who held sway over Marrakech and the surrounding regions from the late 19th to the mid-20th century.

Road across Tizi n'Tinififft towards Zagora from Ouarzazate

Back on the main route, the road cuts a dramatic, ever-winding path through tree-lined gorges and across barren mountainsides before descending to a stony plain. Before you reach Ouarzazate, a surfaced side road leads north to the beautiful kasbah village of Ait Benhaddou. Set prominently upon an island of golden-brown rock fringed by palms and skirted by the small Wadi Melah River, it has been used as a location for many movies, including *Gladiator* and *Lawrence of Arabia*.

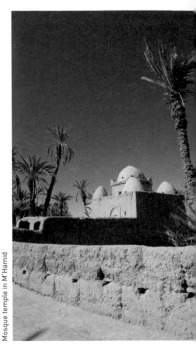

Mosque temple in M'Hamid

The Drâa Valley near Zagora

Driving along desert tracks

Although Ouarzazate is a major crossroads for routes to the Drâa and Dades valleys, it is little more than an obvious place to overnight, with a good selection of hotels. As you drive from here to Zagora, crossing a range of rocky, layered hills at Tizi n'Tinififft, you will begin to see the effect the Drâa's waters have on the desert as verdant palmeries cut a swathe of leafy green through the brown landscape. En route, you will be hard-pressed to decide which of the many kasbahs to visit and which to admire from afar. Just past the market town of Agdz, the fortified walls of the *ksour* at Tamnougalt, with its castle and village, dominate the surrounding countryside. A five-minute drive down a dirt track will take you there. Although the castle has fallen into disrepair, it is possible to get into it via a heavy wooden door if you want to explore its rubble-strewn colonnaded courtyards. The nearby village, where you will see men in hooded cloaks riding donkeys, dates back to the 16th century and its labyrinthine alleyways make for a fascinating wander.

A detour worth considering, especially if you have time to go trekking, heads north-east from Tansikht to Nkob for about 30 km. The road goes between the black, brooding hulk of the volcanic Djebel Sarho – popular with hikers during the winter months when the High Atlas are snowbound and cold – and the dramatic, table-top island peaks of Djebel Rhart. Along the way there are some wonderful isolated kasbahs.

Zagora, set amid a vast palmery, was at the western end of the major trans-Saharan camel caravan route to Timbuktu (Timbouctou in French), the fabled trading centre in Mali. At the far end of the town is a freshly painted sign pointing out that for camels, at least, getting there takes 52 days. Making the journey is not possible as the Moroccan border with Algeria is presently closed. Zagora is a good place to overnight as, further south, hotel options become more limited.

Almost 30 km from Zagora, you will see the first real sand dunes of any size at the settlement of Tinfou. Adjacent to a kasbah-turned-

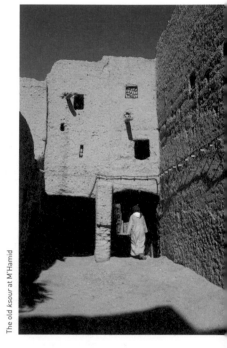

The old *ksour* at M'Hamid

Camel herder near M'Hamid

Camel riding on the Tinfou dunes

Erg Chagaga dunes at sunset

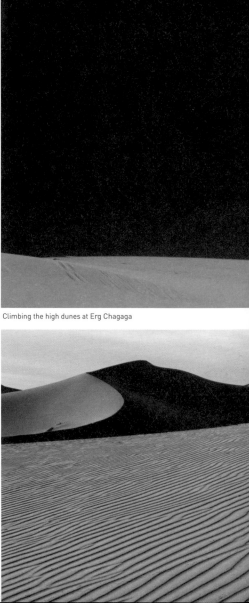

Climbing the high dunes at Erg Chagaga

Mud-walled kasbah near Zagora

Patterns in the sand on the Erg Chagaga dunes

Camel herder on the Tinfou dunes

hotel, it rises impressively from the otherwise flat stony plain, and Berber tribesmen dressed in their traditional blue robes offer short camel rides around it. However, this is not really the Sahara of popular dreams. For this you have to drive the additional 70 km to M'Hamid – an essential last leg of your trip because about 60 km beyond the small town, and reached by four-wheel drive or camel, lie the endless, golden sand dunes of Erg Chagaga. Camping out there

Sunrise at Erg Chagaga dunes

Starry dawn sky at Erg Chagaga camp

among the dunes, seeing wild camels, hearing the silence of the desert and watching the sunset will leave you enchanted by the spirit of the Sahara.

(i) ⋯⋯⋯

Most major international car rental companies have desks at Marrakech airport. Try to get to your destinations before it gets dark, as the scores of unlit people, cycles, donkey carts and even cars make night-time driving a hazardous proposition. There are fuel stations en route, especially in the major towns of Ouarzazate and Zagora, but keep an eye on your fuel gauge. After Zagora, as you head south to the Sahara, there is very limited access to fuel so fill up before you go. In M'Hamid, Sahara Services is a reputable tour company that offers a full range of desert adventures from four-wheel drives to camel excursions, to Erg Chagaga and other dunes. It also offers all-inclusive three- to five-day tours to the desert from Marrakech and Casablanca, if you want to avoid driving.

Sunset over the dunes at Erg Chagaga

Shackleton's voyage
Antarctica

The white continent, encased in eternal ice that reaches a thickness of 4000 metres; the greatest desert and last true wilderness on the planet, where the sun doesn't shine for three months in winter and doesn't set for three months in summer, where storms rage and silence reigns. A voyage to Antarctica is perhaps the ultimate adventure journey.

The region is confusingly tagged with many names, including the South Pole, the Antarctic Circle, the Antarctic Continent and the Antarctic Peninsula. While strictly speaking they are different geographical

Penguin colony at Salisbury Plain, South Georgia

Explorer II anchored among the icebergs at Cuverville Island

Sailing into Salisbury Plain, South Georgia

boundaries and locations, it is commonly understood that they refer to the vast expanse of ice-covered land at the Earth's southern extremity. Although it is possible to go there from several countries, the most popular departure port is Ushaia, the southernmost city in the world, which teeters on the very edge of Argentine Patagonia.

An increasing number of ships sail to Antarctica, and the options available range from a direct there-and-back trip to a more in-depth itinerary that takes you east to the Falkland Islands and then on to South Georgia before cruising south-west to the Antarctic Peninsula.

King penguins on early morning guard at Gold Harbour, South Georgia

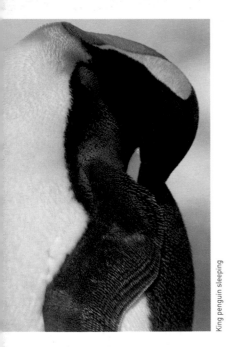

King penguin sleeping

The latter, which is spectacular in its variety, is around 3400 nautical miles and takes two weeks given reasonable weather conditions. The seas can be the wildest on the planet and, while you would be unfortunate if they were very rough for the entire voyage, you need to expect some tossing and pitching en route.

After leaving Ushaia the ship, the *Explorer II*, sails via the dramatic Beagle Channel, which threads between the mountainous Patagonian mainland and a string of islands, into the Drake Passage – which is notorious for providing the roughest parts of the voyage. However, at these latitudes it is the luck of the draw and you may escape with just a gentle rolling. After a day and a half at sea, you arrive at Port Stanley on the Falkland Islands. A colourful array of houses and the notable Christ Church Cathedral, with its whalebone archway, line the shoreline and a short ride on one of the ship's Zodiac boats takes you to the jetty. The Falkland Islands came to international attention in 1982 when the United Kingdom and Argentina fought over their sovereignty, and the legacies of that conflict are visible around the many battlefield sites. This is also the first opportunity to see penguins, which are reached via an exciting trip in a four-wheel-drive vehicle across exposed hillsides.

In the evening you depart for South Georgia, a two-day sail across the Scotia Sea. Although not as infamous as the Drake Passage, the waters here can be equally wild, and most passengers will feel the effects to some degree if huge swells roll under the *Explorer II*. When the seas calm down, it is fascinating to stand at the stern and watch the spectacular flying displays of the numerous seabirds, including albatrosses, that follow the ship. And it is a thrilling moment when the first iceberg is spotted – an excitement surpassed only by the sighting of the first whales. With clear skies, and providing you can get yourself out of bed at 4 a.m., you may be treated to a glorious sunrise upon arrival at the mountainous island of South Georgia.

Before the voyage, most people expect that Antarctica will be the highlight of the journey, but South Georgia often ends up being their

King penguins on the beach at Salisbury Plain, South Georgia

Weddel seals fighting

favourite place. It is one of the world's truly magical locations, isolated and yet crammed full of incredible wildlife and rugged scenery. Over two days the ship calls into bays such as Salisbury Plain, Gold Harbour and Larsen Harbour, and takes you to the historic Grytviken settlement. A whaling station from 1904 to the mid-1960s, Grytviken is the final resting place of Sir Ernest Shackleton. With five of his men he rowed the lifeboat *James Caird* 1300 km to South Georgia from Elephant Island where the rest of his crew were stranded – they had rowed there after HMS *Endurance* was crushed by the ice further south.

In magnificent Gold Harbour, backdropped by the blue ice of the high, hanging Bertrab glacier, the beach is alive with thousands of king penguins and their fluffy brown chicks, and with many species of seal, including the monstrous elephant and fur seals. Disembarking from the Zodiacs is like walking into your very own wildlife documentary, especially when the dominant male elephant seals, known as the beach masters, decide to warn off rival males with dramatic, lumbering charges. In the afternoon, the ship sails past the Heaney glacier and pulls into Drygalski Fjord for a Zodiac tour up the adjoining Larsen Harbour, edged by towering cliffs.

Seals, like this one in Gold Harbour, spend most of the day lazing

Glacier at the head of the Drygalski Fjord, South Georgia

Geothermal hot springs at Whaler's Bay, Deception Island

Fur seals can be very aggressive defending their territory

Albatross taking off in the Beagle Channel

Space is limited on the beach at Gold Harbour

Sunrise at Gold Harbour, South Georgia

Curious king penguin chicks

Point Wild on Elephant Island

Afternoon light in the Gerlache Strait

A further two days' sailing, over very rough seas, leads to Elephant Island and a call into Point Wild. The windswept spit, surrounded by soaring rock islands, is a daunting place even for a few hours. It is beyond comprehension that Frank Wild, who was left in charge by Shackleton, and after whom Point Wild is named, managed to maintain morale among the men who made camp there for four months, and ensured they all survived.

The next stop is Deception Island, where the ship passes through the narrow Neptune's Bellows into the flooded crater of a volcano. At the old Hektor whaling station geothermal springs beneath the beach, which is made of volcanic ash, create a series of steaming pools of hot water in which hardy travellers can swim.

Overnight, *Explorer II* sails into and through the beautiful, iceberg-strewn Gerlache Strait, heading for Cuverville Island, home to thousands of gentoo penguins, and then for Neko Harbour on the Antarctic Peninsula itself. The moment you step on to land will be a memorable one. And the stunning, ice-laden bay, its calm waters

Dusk over the harbour at Grytviken, South Georgia

Sunrise over South Georgia

reflecting the enormous, crevasse-ridden, ice-blue glaciers above, is a fitting place to end your visit to what is, without doubt, the most spectacular and pristine continent on the planet. A final two days' sailing takes you back across the Drake Passage to Ushaia – where you will probably yearn for the world of ice you've left behind.

ⓘ ┈┈

Explorer II, which can be booked through Abercrombie & Kent, is one of about 30 ships that sail to Antarctica. Ushaia is reached via flights from Buenos Aires in Argentina, or Santiago in Chile. British Airways flies to Buenos Aires, and Aerolineas Argentina flies to Ushaia from there. Abercrombie & Kent will arrange flights if required. It is essential to take plenty of warm clothing; several thin layers are better than one or two thick ones. Passengers on *Explorer II* are given warm waterproof jackets as part of the package. Wellington boots are also essential as you will get wet during the Zodiac landings. Full briefings are given on board about how to behave around the wildlife. It is totally forbidden to remove anything from any of the places where you land. Daily lectures add significantly to the Antarctic experience. The itinerary and ports of call are all subject to change, depending on weather conditions. Take a flexible mindset.

International airlines

Air Canada
www.aircanada.com

British Airways
www.ba.com

Qantas
www.qantas.com

Scandinavian Airlines
www.sas.se

Riding the Okavango Delta, Botswana

African Horseback Safaris
www.africanhorseback.com
Tel: +267 686 3154

Tim Best Travel
www.timbesttravel.com
Tel: +44 (0)20 7591 0300

Ice cap trek, Argentina

Oyikil Viajes
www.oyikilviajes.com.ar
Tel: +54 11 4700 0020

Journey Latin America
www.journeylatinamerica.co.uk
Tel: +44 (0)20 8747 8315

Santa Cruz – Patagonia Tourism
www.santacruz.gov.ar

Art Hotel, Buenos Aires
www.arthotel.com.ar
Tel: +54 11 4821 6248

Hotel Posada Los Alamos,
El Calafate
www.posadalosalamos.com
Tel: +54 02902 491 144

Along the Gibb River Road, Australia

Tourism Western Australia
www.westernaustralia.com
Tel: +61 8 9262 1700

Hertz – Broome Airport
www.hertz.com
Tel: +61 8 9192 1428

Canal du Midi, France

French Tourist Office
www.franceguide.com

Driving along Route 66, USA

Arizona Office of Tourism
www.arizonaguide.com

Following the reindeer migration, Sweden

Vägvisaren – Pathfinder Lapland
www.pathfinderlapland.se
Tel: +46 970 555 60

Nature's Best
www.naturensbasta.se
Tel: +46 647 660 025

Swedish Travel & Tourism Council
www.visit-sweden.com

Kiruna and Lapland Tourist Office
www.lappland.se

Hotell Vinterpalatset, Kiruna
www.vinterpalatset.se
Tel: +46 980 67770

The Silk Route, China/Uzbekistan

China National Tourist Office
www.cnto.org

Uzbekistan Tourism
www.uzbektourism.uz

Tracking mountain gorillas, Rwanda

Discovery Initiatives
www.discoveryinitiatives.co.uk
Tel: +44 (0)1285 643333

Yukon river journey, Canada

Tourism Yukon
www.touryukon.com

Kanoe People
www.kanoepeople.com
Tel: +1 867 668 4899

Tracing the life of Gaudí, Spain

Spanish Tourist Board
www.spain.info

Orissan tribal journey, India

Dove Tours
www.dovetours.com
Tel: +91 674 254 7175

India Tourist Office
www.incredibleindia.org

A tall-ship voyage, Italy

Star Clippers (UK reservations)
www.starclippers.co.uk
Tel: +44 (0)1473 292029

Star Clippers (rest of world
reservations)
www.starclippers.com
Tel: +377 9797 8400 (Europe)
Tel: +1 305 442 0550 (USA)

Journey to the Sounds of Wine, New Zealand

Tourism New Zealand
www.newzealand.com

Sea kayaking cays, the Bahamas

Bahamas Ministry of Tourism
www.bahamas.co.uk

Starfish
www.kayakbahamas.com
Tel: +242 336 3033

Peace & Plenty Inn, George Town
www.peaceandplenty.com
Tel: +242 336 2551

By rail through Copper Canyon, Mexico

Mexico Tourism Board
www.visitmexico.com

Chihuahua State Tourism
www.coppercanyon-mexico.com
Tel: +011 52 1 410 1077

Chepe Railway
www.chepe.com.mx

Hotel San Francisco, Chihuahua
www.hotelsanfrancisco.com.mx
Tel: +52 614 439 9000
Tel: 1 800 847 2546 (toll free
from USA)

Hotel Divisadero Barrancas,
Divisadero
www.hoteldivisadero.com
Tel: +52 614 415 1199
Tel: 1 800 226 9661 (toll free
from USA)

Hotel Posada del Hidalgo, El Fuerte
www.hotelposadadelhidalgo.com
Tel: +52 698 893 0242

Horse-drawn caravan, Ireland

Clissmann Horse Caravans
www.clissmann.com/wicklow/
Tel: +353 404 48188

Irish Ferries
www.irishferries.com
Tel: +44 (0)8705 171717

Tourism Ireland
www.tourismireland.com

Into the ice bear kingdom, Canada

Discover the World
www.discovertheworld.co.uk
Tel: +44 (0)1737 218 800

Hudson Bay Helicopters
www.hudsonbayheli.com
Tel. +1 204 675 2576

Churchill Motel, Churchill
Tel: +1 204 675 8853

The Fort Garry Hotel, Winnipeg
www.fortgarryhotel.com
Tel: +1 204 942 8251
Tel: +1 800 665 8088 (toll free)

A Bohemian journey, Czech Republic

Thomsonfly
www.thomsonfly.com
Tel: +44 (0)870 1900 737

HotelClub
www.hotelclub.com

Paddles and pedals, Costa Rica

Coast to Coast Adventures
www.ctocadventures.com
Tel: +506 280 8054

Through Patagonian fjords, Chile

Navimag
www.navimag.com

Walking with Wordsworth, England

Cumbria Tourist Board
www.golakes.co.uk

Trans-Mongolian Railway, Russia/Mongolia/China

Trans-Siberian – The Russian
Experience
www.trans-siberian.co.uk

China National Tourist Office
www.cnto.org

Driving through fall colours, USA

New Hampshire Travel and
Tourism
www.visitnh.gov

Vermont Tourism & Marketing
www.travel-vermont.com

The Foliage Network
www.foliagenetwork.com

On the *Road to Mandalay*, Myanmar

Orient Express
www.orient-express.com
Tel: +44 (0)845 077 2222 (UK)

The Governor's Residence Hotel,
Yangon
www.pansea.com
Tel: +95 1 229 860

Driving the Uyuni Salt Flat, Bolivia

Andean Summits, La Paz
www.andeansummits.com
Tel: +591 2 242 2106

The Eastern & Oriental Express, Singapore/Thailand

Orient Express
www.orient-express.com
Tel: +44 (0)845 077 2222 (UK)

Camino de Santiago, Spain

Spanish Tourist Board
www.spain.info

La Ruta Maya, Mexico/ Guatemala/Honduras

Mexico Tourism Board
www.visitmexico.com

Guatemala Tourism Commission
www.visitguatemala.com

Honduran Tourism Board
www.letsgohonduras.com

Into the Sahara, Morocco

Moroccan National Tourist Office
www.visitmorocco.com

The Best of Morocco
www.morocco-travel.com
Tel: +44 (0)1380 828533

Sahara Services
Tel: +212 (0)61 776766
www.saharaservices.info

Shackleton's voyage, Antarctica

Abercrombie & Kent
www.abercrombiekent.co.uk
Tel: +44 (0)845 0700 600

Acknowledgements

Steve would like to thank his mum, Dilys, and sister, Mel, and Clare would like to thank her mum and dad, Elaine and Owen, for all their unwavering support and helping them to see light at the end of the tunnel during this extensive project.

Steve and Clare would in particular like to thank Nicky Ross, Christopher Tinker, Stuart Cooper, Kenneth McKay and Laura Nickoll at BBC Worldwide, Bobby Birchall at DW Design, Tessa Clark and Vicki Vrint for their invaluable work in bringing this book together. They would also like to thank Malie Rich-Griffith, Dave Willis and Paul Deegan for their photographic contributions.

No travel is ever done alone, so they would also like to thank the following for their support, advice and assistance with organizing trips, making the journeys more enjoyable and generally keeping them sane during the hectic schedule: Neil Rogers; María Zivkovic and Alberto Bilotte at Oyikil Viajes; Andres their guide in Patagonia; Larry Hobbs, Jannie Cloete, Giovanni Biasutti, Charlie Wheatley, Jason Hicks, Phillip Hicks, Chris Simpson, Bob Burton, Martin Almqvist, David and Debbie Pain, Penny and Grace Porterfield and the *Explorer II* crew in Antarctica; Sara Rogers and Matilda Granville at Abercrombie & Kent; Martin Petts, Sarah Barnett and Dee Byrne at BGB Communications; Caroline Grayburn at Tim Best Travel; Sarah-Jane Gullick, Corne du Plessis, Pam McLean, Bongwe, Dany Hancock and Malise Scott-Barrett in Botswana; Lennart Pittja and family in Lapland; Emelie Klein at the Swedish Tourism Council; Lupita Ayala at the Mexico Tourism Board; Gillian Monahan at Tourism New Zealand; Javier and José at Andean Summits in La Paz; Jeffrey Rayner at Star Clippers; Wilko, Judith, Koen, Jack Weishahn and the Gabor fan club; Dick Jones; Alexis Thornely at Discover the World; Chris Johnston and Julian Matthews at Discovery Initiatives; Mary Clissman and her team in Wicklow; Alun and Irene Newby; Suzie and Lydie; Anna Nash at Orient Express; the *Road to Mandalay* crew; Phil Nelson at Surf-Lines; Palm Equipment, Tom Hutton and Keith Byrne at The North Face for keeping us warm and dry and to the countless other people we shared time with on our travels.

First published 2006
Reprinted 2006 (three times)

Text copyright © Steve Watkins and Clare Jones 2006
The moral right of the authors has been asserted.

All images are © Steve Watkins and Clare Jones / www.vividplanet.com except the following:
pp.60–5 (all) © Malie Rich-Griffith/infocusphotos.com; pp.168–70 (all), 172 (both) © Dave Willis/Mountain Sport Photography; p.176 © Nikolai Ignatiev/Network; p.178 (all), 179 (bottom), 181–3 (all) © Paul Deegan; p.179 (top) © John James/Alamy; p.180 (bottom) © DIOMEDIA/Alamy

ISBN-13: 978 0 563 52263 8
ISBN-10: 0 563 52263 1

Published by BBC Books, BBC Worldwide Ltd, Woodlands, 80 Wood Lane, London W12 0TT

Commissioning editor: Nicky Ross
Project editor: Christopher Tinker
Copy-editor: Tessa Clark
Designer: Bobby Birchall (DW Design)
Production controller: Kenneth McKay

Set in DIN Regular
Colour origination and printing by Butler & Tanner Ltd, Frome, England